Easy Baking from Scratch

D1401463

Easy BAKING

FROM SCRATCH

Quick Tutorials ✳ **Time-Saving Tips**
Extraordinary Sweet and Savory Classics

EILEEN GRAY

ROCKRIDGE
PRESS

For general information on our other products and services or to obtain technical support, please contact our Customer Care Department within the U.S. at (866) 744-2665, or outside the U.S. at (510) 253-0500.

Rockridge Press publishes its books in a variety of electronic and print formats. Some content that appears in print may not be available in electronic books, and vice versa.

Designers: Alyssa Nassner (cover), Liz Cosgrove and Katy Brown (interior)
Editor: Kim Suarez
Production Editor: Andrew Yackira

Photography © Marjia Vidal, Food styling by Cregg Green. Author photo courtesy of Campli Photo (campliphoto.com)

ISBN: Print 978-1-64152-105-5 | eBook 978-1-64152-106-2

For Michèl, my rock and the world's greatest husband, for always supporting me as I follow my dreams.

For my mom, for all the bragging you do.

Contents

Introduction

Just about everyone loves baked goods. But even better than eating homemade cookies still warm from the oven is sharing them with grateful family and friends. Whenever my now-grown children come to visit, I bake their favorite treats to welcome them home.

Baking isn't just about the food; it's also a way to create bonds with those around you. Everyone appreciates something you baked especially for them, even if it's not perfect. For sure, food is much more than a way to fill the belly. Food is culture, food is love, and food is the stuff of childhood memories. Bring your child into the kitchen to bake with you, and those memories become even sweeter.

I know a lot of people who think they can't bake because they aren't used to following a recipe, or they're worried about carefully measuring every ingredient. It is true that for successful baking, you will need to follow a recipe. If the recipe isn't accurate, it doesn't matter how careful you are—it won't work.

Take cooking, for example. You can throw pretty much anything in a pot with water or broth, and it will be soup. It might taste terrible, but you can still call it "soup." On the other hand, you can't just toss together a random amount of flour, a little sugar, and a couple of eggs and assume you'll come out with a cake. You might end up with a giant cracker, or a puddle of greasy goo. Maybe that's why some folks, even many who are excellent cooks, are a little afraid of baking. But I've got some reassurance for you: Baking is easier than it might seem, and I'm here to give you the know-how!

Although baking requires a bit of measuring and recipe following, the best way to become a better baker is to keep practicing. Baking is a skill and a science, but it's not rocket science. If you have a good, reliable recipe to start with, you are halfway to baking success. Follow the instructions, and you'll be amazed at your results. Over time, you can learn how to get away with some hacks and shortcuts—and I'll even teach you some.

To get you started, or even to help you advance your baking, I'm happy to share these quick tutorials, time-saving tips, culinary tricks, and well-tested recipes I've developed over my 30 years of professional baking. But believe me, you don't need the skills of a pastry chef to create these recipes.

Chapter 1 is a crash course to get you started. I'll tell you exactly which ingredients and equipment you'll need to set up a baker's kitchen. Read through my "baker's dozen" essential checklist. Use these universal tips whenever you're baking to ensure great results. When you're ready to start baking, jump to chapters 2 through 8. There you'll find more than 100 easy-to-follow recipes I've created for baked goods, which are sure to impress your friends and family. Many of the basics are covered in this book, including things like blueberry muffins, brownies, snickerdoodles, sandwich bread, and good old apple pie.

And then there are the cakes. For 10 years, I owned and operated an award-winning custom cake business. I've adapted my best recipes from this business for the home baker with easy-to-find ingredients and simple instructions. You'll learn how to make my super-tender Vanilla Butter Cake (page 76), Old-Fashioned Chocolate Cake (page 78), and the best Carrot Cake ever (page 81). I'll even teach you a special mixing method for creating melt-in-your-mouth cakes.

After that, I'll help you broaden your baking horizons. Think you can't make homemade croissants or puff pastry? You can *totally* do it with my step-by-step instructions!

If you don't have a sweet tooth, check out the entire chapter called Savory Baked Goods (page 199), which includes favorites like pizza dough, focaccia, and biscuits, as well as my special Zucchini & Ricotta Pie (page 213) and healthy Oatmeal Crispbread (page 203).

Finally, this book sails beyond US shores for inspiration. In these pages you'll find Empanadas (page 222), Dutch Apple Tart (page 128), Pita Bread (page 180), Pithiviers (page 147), Baklava (page 161), and more. I even share my special recipe for Raisin Scones (page 25), which is British mom–approved and has been one of my most popular recipes for more than 20 years.

Beyond this cookbook, I have a blog called Baking Sense, and do you know what that name means to me? Well, I have found that if you bake often enough, you begin to get a sense for things, like how a good dough should feel and when something is precisely ready to come out of the oven. Make that cookie recipe a few times and you'll just know when the butter and sugar are getting fluffy, and smell when the almonds are perfectly toasted.

I am certain that baking is not an innate talent, like something you either have or you don't. Baking is a skill that you can develop by trial and, yes, some errors. The good news is that the best way to develop a "baking sense" is simply by baking.

So, let's get started!

CHOCOLATE CHIP COOKIES *page 43*

Chapter 1

THE ESSENTIAL GUIDE TO EASY BAKING

Indeed, baking is culture; it's tradition; it's comfort and celebration. And it's something we get better at with practice. As beginners, however, we can set ourselves up for success. The best springboard to success is preparation. We need the baking trifecta: good recipes, high-quality ingredients, and the right tools. In this chapter, we will explore these areas and the role each one plays in helping us consistently create and present excellent dishes, resplendent in all of their intended attributes, textures, colors, and flavors.

Baking is easier, and the results are best, when you have the proper tools and ingredients. In a perfect world, we'd all have kitchens equipped with every tool and gourmet ingredient that our heart desires. In the real world, most of us have space and budget limitations to consider. In this chapter I'll share which tools and ingredients I've found essential for baking, which ones are easy and inexpensive add-ons, and which fun stuff you might want to put on your "wish list."

ESSENTIAL EQUIPMENT

None of the recipes in this book require fancy gadgets or appliances. But every kitchen should contain some basic equipment for easy baking. Eventually, as you continue baking, you might find that some of those "wish list" tools become must-haves for you. In the meantime, don't forget that your best tool is a pair of clean hands—it's okay to touch the dough!

Cookware & Bakeware

MUST-HAVE

Baking pan (9-by-13-inch) You can use this pan to bake brownies, bar cookies, and single-layer cakes. A nonstick version makes cleanup a breeze.

Deep-dish pie plate I like glass pie plates for baking sweet and savory pies. Glass retains heat for a nice brown crust.

Loaf pan A 9-by-5-inch loaf pan is the standard vessel for baking sandwich breads, pound cakes, and quick breads. Get a nonstick loaf pan to make life easier.

Rimmed baking sheets If you can, get two. You'll use these large sheets for baking everything from cookies to sheet cakes to pizza. Rimless cookie sheets are handy for cookies and biscuits, but if you must choose one or the other, rimmed baking sheets are more versatile.

Round cake pans I recommend having at least two (8-inch) cake pans for baking layer cakes.

Standard cupcake pan A pan that bakes a dozen standard-size cupcakes or muffins is essential. Jumbo and mini muffin pans are nice extras.

EASY EXTRAS

Bundt pan This specialty pan has a hole in the middle and a ridged surface for quick and even baking of cakes and monkey breads. The standard size is a 12-cup volume.

Cast iron skillet You might already have one of these heavy, durable pans in the house for cooking meat and potatoes. A cast iron skillet is also wonderful for making upside-down cakes, tarts, and cobblers.

Fluted tart pan A shallow tart pan with fluted edges and a removable bottom will allow you to make gorgeous fruit tarts that look like they came from a fancy pastry shop.

WISH LIST

Springform pan Because it has a spring-release side, a springform pan makes easy work of unmolding cheese-cakes and other fragile baked goods.

Square pan (9-inch) This is a good pan for making half batches of brownies or snack cakes and other treats. A pan that is nonstick and has a fitted lid is especially nice.

Tools & Utensils

MUST-HAVE

Hand whisk You'll need a hand whisk for combining dry ingredients and folding together light and airy batters. With some effort, you can also use a hand whisk for whipping egg whites or heavy cream if you don't have an electric hand mixer.

Liquid and dry measuring cups Glass or plastic cups are used for measuring liquid ingredients. You can see the measurement at eye level from the outside of the cup. Nested, scoop-style cups are used for measuring dry ingredients with the "dip and sweep" method (see page 10).

Measuring spoons A good set that measures from ¼ teaspoon to 1 tablespoon will serve you well. The spoons you eat with are not the proper size for measuring ingredients.

Mixing bowls An assortment of bowls in an assortment of sizes (some microwave-safe) makes measuring and mixing recipes easy and efficient.

Silicone spatulas Spatulas are handy for mixing batters and for cleanly scraping batter as you transfer it from bowl to pan. Silicone spatulas are heat-resistant.

EASY EXTRAS

Cookie scoops Spring-release scoops come in a variety of sizes and make it easy to quickly portion cookies, muffins, cream puffs, and even meatballs with precision.

Mesh sieve There is no need for a special flour sifter. You can use a simple mesh sieve for sifting dry ingredients. You can also use a sieve to strain custards, fruit purées, and liquids.

Offset spatulas These come in a variety of sizes and are useful for spreading cake batter, icing cakes, and lifting cookies. If you only get one, the small 4.5-inch spatula is the most versatile and useful. The 7.75-inch spatula is perfect for icing cakes.

Parchment paper and/or silicone baking mat These are in the easy extras section, but for me they are must-haves. Butter and flour are messy and can stain a baking pan. Parchment or a silicone baking mat makes cleanup easy and also prevents cookies from spreading too much.

Rasp grater This useful and inexpensive tool is used to finely grate citrus zest and fresh nutmeg.

Rolling pin You'll want a rolling pin to roll pie dough, cookie dough, and bread dough. My favorite is a tapered French rolling pin made from wood.

Round biscuit cutters Sure, it's possible to cut out cookies and biscuits with the rim of a glass, but a biscuit cutter will cut through dough more easily, making a cleaner cut. A nested set comes with several sizes.

WISH LIST

Bench scraper This rectangular stainless-steel tool with a plastic handle is great for portioning dough, icing cakes, and cleaning your work surface.

Cake turntable I can't help this one—I owned a cake shop. This tool makes it so easy to ice a cake like a pro and crimp a beautiful piecrust. Use the turntable to cut perfect cake layers, and then you can make a torted (multilayered) cake that looks like it came from a high-end bakery.

Pastry bag and tips Reusable or disposable pastry bags are great for piping cookies and éclairs, or for decorating cakes. A round tip and star tip are the most useful for piping cookies and applying basic decorations.

Appliances

MUST-HAVE

Electric mixer A handheld mixer with beaters (and perhaps a whisk option) is needed for mixing cookie doughs, cake batters, and icings. While it's technically possible to mix most batters and doughs by hand, this inexpensive appliance makes baking much easier, quicker, and, admittedly, more pleasant.

EASY EXTRAS

Food processor This appliance makes quick work of chopping nuts, puréeing fruits, or blending batters. You can even use many processors for mixing bread dough and piecrust dough.

Kitchen scale The most accurate way to measure ingredients for baking is with a kitchen scale. A digital scale that can measure pounds, ounces, and grams is great to have. I always list my recipes with both volume and weight measures. All professional bakers use weight measures because precision is rewarded with consistent results. Why shouldn't home bakers reap the same rewards?

WISH LIST

Stand mixer Its large capacity and strong motor make a stand mixer a worthwhile investment for a baker's kitchen. A heavy-duty mixer can knead bread dough, make quick work of whipping meringue, and effortlessly cream cookie dough. Some stand mixers have attachments for making pasta, spiralizing vegetables, or grinding meats and grains.

Essential Ingredients

Cookies, cakes, and pies are only as good as the ingredients used to make them. I can't stress enough how important it is to purchase quality ingredients, and to use the ingredients listed in the recipe without making random substitutions (see page 12 to learn how to swap ingredients in a pinch). To get you started, I've listed the basic ingredients that are required for almost all baking projects. You probably already have some of these ingredients in your home. Beyond the basics, there are ingredients that you might not always keep on hand but that are easy to find. You'll want to purchase these ingredients when you're planning to make a specific recipe that calls for them. At the end of this list are some very special pastry ingredients that you don't need for everyday baking but are fun to try out for special-occasion treats.

MUST-HAVE

Baking powder This is the leavening agent you'll use most often. Baking powder can be stored at room temperature and should be used before the expiration date. "Double-acting" baking powder releases carbon dioxide twice: first when wet ingredients are added to the batter, and a second time when the batter meets the heat of the oven. Generally, you'll need 1 teaspoon of baking powder for each cup of flour in a recipe.

NO TWO OVENS ARE ALIKE

All baking books list specific oven temperatures and baking times for each recipe. However, those temperatures and times are estimates based on the oven that was used for recipe testing. Since no two ovens are alike, the baking time in your oven may vary from the estimated time by more than a few minutes. The best way to be sure you're baking at the right temperature is to purchase an inexpensive oven thermometer. Use the thermometer to test the temperature on all the racks, in the front and the back, and on both sides. By doing this, you'll find out if you have any "hot spots" in your oven.

Baking soda This ingredient is used in recipes that contain an acidic ingredient such as sour cream or yogurt. Baking soda can be stored at room temperature and should be used before the expiration date. Generally, you'll need about ¼ teaspoon of baking soda for each cup of flour in a recipe.

Butter This product contributes moisture and tenderizes a baked good, and, of course, it has an incomparable flavor. The default butter for baking is unsalted. Some recipes will call for shortening, lard, or even oil instead of butter. Generally, shortening can be swapped 1:1 for butter, but butter and oil are not usually interchangeable in a recipe without making an adjustment to the liquid in that recipe.

Chocolate Ah, chocolate. It contributes happiness to our lives, and flavor, fat, and sometimes sugar to baked goods. The percentage listed on the package refers to the percentage of cocoa solids in the chocolate. The higher the percentage, the less sugar in the chocolate. 70 percent chocolate is less sweet than 60 percent chocolate. Additionally, chocolate chips are not a substitute for semisweet chocolate, since chocolate chips have stabilizers that change the texture. And while you're welcome to use white chocolate in your chocolate chip cookie recipe, it is not true chocolate because it doesn't have any cocoa solids. White chocolate is a mixture of cocoa butter, sugar, and milk solids.

Cocoa powder This ingredient contributes flavor and some structure to a baked good. Most recipes will specify either "Dutch process" or natural cocoa. Natural cocoa powder is lighter in color and is acidic. Dutch process indicates the cocoa has been alkalized, which makes it darker in color, less acidic, and less bitter. The two types of cocoa are generally interchangeable.

Eggs These contribute to the structure of a baked good and provide moisture. Most recipes assume the use of grade A large eggs. Kept in an airtight container in the refrigerator, eggs will stay fresh for several weeks. Once out of the shell, they should be used right away or frozen. Yes, you can freeze whole eggs, yolks, or whites. Egg whites can be frozen as they are, but to prevent freezer burn to yolks, mix in 1 teaspoon of salt or 1 tablespoon of sugar for each cup of egg yolks. Whole eggs require ½ teaspoon of salt or 1½ teaspoons of sugar per cup to prevent freezer burn.

Flour This base ingredient contains the protein gluten, which helps form the structure of baked goods. For bakers, it's essential to understand the three flours you'll use most: bread flour, all-purpose flour, and cake flour. Bread flour has the most gluten, and cake flour has the least. All-purpose flour has medium gluten content.

Use high-gluten bread flour for strong breads, and soft cake flour for tender cakes. If you only keep one type of flour on hand, all-purpose is your best bet. Whole-grain flours include the bran and the germ, and they form a weaker structure than white flour.

Salt Salt contributes flavor, and used in large enough quantities, it can affect the texture of a baked good. Without salt, most baked goods would taste flat. Unless otherwise specified, assume that the salt called for in a recipe is table salt. Since the crystal sizes are different, table salt, kosher salt, and sea salt are not interchangeable by volume.

Sugar This sweet ingredient adds flavor to baked goods and makes them tender and moist. The one sugar you should have on hand is white granulated sugar.

White and brown sugar differ in that brown sugar contains molasses. Confectioners' sugar is white sugar that is ground to a finer texture. You don't want to use confectioners' sugar in recipes that use the "creaming" method, since it's the crystals in granulated sugar that help whip air into the butter for light and airy cakes and cookies.

Vanilla extract This is the most common flavoring in baked goods. Real vanilla is made by soaking vanilla beans in alcohol to extract the flavor. Vanilla extract lasts virtually forever in the pantry. I only recommend using real vanilla extract, not imitation vanilla extract, because the former has a full, real vanilla flavor.

EASY EXTRAS

Buttermilk This is a wonderful baking ingredient. It has a special flavor, and its acidity tenderizes baked goods. The best alternative to buttermilk is buttermilk powder, which will keep for several years in the pantry.

Chocolate chips These morsels are used for their famous namesake cookies, of course, but can also be folded into cakes, quick breads, and pies.

Cornstarch Made from corn, this ingredient thickens custards and can replace some of the flour in a recipe. It keeps indefinitely, so it's worth having in the pantry.

Cream cheese This ingredient makes a delicious icing for carrot cake and can also be used to make pie doughs and cheesecakes.

Heavy cream Only heavy cream can be used for making whipped cream. Unless otherwise specified, assume that "cream" means heavy cream. Because of its high fat content, cream is also used to make luxurious custards and mousses.

Liquor A little will go a long way, and you might not even taste the liquor itself in the finished product; it often just makes the other flavors taste better. Liquor can also be used as a prominent flavor in recipes like Rum Cake (page 89).

Milk Unless otherwise specified, use whole milk for baking. In a pinch, low-fat milk is generally okay to use. Milk adds liquid, fat, and flavor to a baked good. A good substitute is dried milk powder, reconstituted.

Spices Cinnamon is the most common spice used in baking and well worth keeping in the pantry. Nutmeg, ginger, cloves, and cardamom are also used for baking, but less frequently. It's better to buy a smaller container and replace as needed. If stored in a tightly closed container in a cool, dark place, most spices will keep for a couple of years.

Vegetable shortening This ingredient has a long shelf life and can be used in place of butter in most recipes.

Shortening is a good substitute for butter to create a vegan recipe.

Yeast If you like baking bread, yeast will be a must-have for you. It is a living organism that "eats" the sugars in a dough and then releases carbon dioxide gases to make a baked good rise. Most home bakers use either "active dry" or "instant" yeast. Instant yeast may also be labeled "quick rise" or "rapid rise." One little packet contains 2¼ teaspoons of yeast. Opened yeast should be stored in the refrigerator and used by the expiration date for best results.

WISH LIST

Almond paste This is a product that cannot be made at home. The almonds are crushed under rollers to form a thick paste, which is then mixed with sugar. Almond paste is used to make homemade marzipan, almond petit fours, or a luxurious filling for croissants or tarts.

Exotic spices and extracts You can really go in so many directions with this category—the list is virtually endless. Some of my favorites for baking are rose water, fennel seeds, star anise, grains of paradise, lavender, lemongrass, fresh mint, and mint oil. Spices and extracts give baked goods depth of taste, smell, and appearance—they transport the senses!

Sourdough starter For bread bakers, there is no greater thrill than creating and nurturing a sourdough starter. Not familiar with sourdough starter? An Internet search will lead you through how it's done, as well as through wonderful stories of people who have passed this living thing down through the generations. Sourdough bread is made with no commercial yeast, just the natural yeast that is living in the starter. You can purchase a sourdough starter rather than making one yourself, but at some point, do make one yourself anyway!

Vanilla beans These have a more intense and complex flavor than vanilla extract. To get to the vanilla seeds, you'll split the pod lengthwise and scrape the tiny black seeds out of the pod. Use the seeds in your recipe and save the pod. You can place used vanilla pods in a canister of granulated sugar to make vanilla sugar, or soak them in a jar of vodka to make homemade vanilla extract.

BASIC ALTERNATIVES

For some of us, common baking ingredients may pose a risk due to allergies or other health issues. Other folks choose not to use certain ingredients for lifestyle or religious reasons. Here are a few vegetarian, allergy-friendly, and minimally processed alternatives to common baking ingredients:*

COMMON INGREDIENT	POSSIBLE SUBSTITUTIONS
Butter	Vegetable shortening, vegetable oil, and coconut oil can replace all the butter in a recipe to make it vegan-friendly. Applesauce or prune purée can replace up to half of the butter in a recipe to make a lower-fat version.
Cream/milk	Almond milk, coconut milk, rice milk, and soy milk can be used to make a recipe dairy-free and vegan.
Eggs	Commercial egg replacers can be used instead of whole eggs. Aquafaba (the resulting liquid from cooking beans) can substitute for egg whites.
Wheat flour	Use a premade gluten-free flour, or make your own using a mixture of non-wheat flours and xanthan gum.
White flour	Whole-grain flour can replace up to half of the white flour in most recipes to create a heartier and more nutritious baked good.
Granulated sugar	All sugars are natural and plant-based, but some are more processed than others. Coconut sugar, date sugar, agave syrup, brown rice syrup, honey, and pure maple syrup are some of the sugars that can be used in place of granulated sugar.*

*A simple 1:1 exchange is not always possible. Sometimes the recipe will have to be adapted for the alternative ingredient. For example, using honey to replace granulated sugar would add extra liquid to the recipe, so you'd need to reduce the total amount of liquid in the recipe to make up for the difference.

ESSENTIAL CHECKLIST: THE BAKER'S DOZEN

The following "Baker's Dozen" checklist of techniques is universally helpful for baking success. Before you start any baking project, take a glance at this list to make sure you're on track to make your best baked goods.

1. ***Mise en place,*** which means "everything in place," is a system employed in every professional kitchen and was the first lesson I learned in pastry school. For easy and efficient baking, always read through your recipe, then gather your ingredients and tools before you begin. This helps ensure that you have everything you need to complete the dish. (Picture those cooking shows where the chef has all the bowls of ingredients neatly prepped on the counter.) Practice *mise en place* and you won't find yourself looking for the sugar while your egg whites are over-whipping.

2. **Preheat the oven,** and if you have one with a convection setting, use that when appropriate. If you put your cake, bread, or cookies in an underheated oven, they might not rise or spread properly. The convection setting is great for items that bake fast or when you want good browning. Lower the oven temperature by 25°F when using convection.

3. **Prep the baking pan.** Nothing is more frustrating than having your beautiful cake or bread hopelessly stuck in the pan. It's also frustrating to witness your cookies spreading too thin because the pan was buttered when it shouldn't have been. Follow the directions to be sure you're preparing your pan appropriately.

4. **"Dip and sweep" dry ingredients.** This method is preferred if you're not using a kitchen scale to weigh your ingredients. Using a proper dry measuring cup, dip the cup into the bag of flour to fill, then sweep away the excess so you have a level cup of flour.

5. **Temper** ingredients according to the recipe. For baking, this is often room temperature. Room temperature is 65° to 70°F.

6. **Sift and/or whisk** the dry ingredients as specified in the recipe. Sifting not only aerates the flour, it also removes lumps and mixes the ingredients. Whisking dry ingredients ensures that the salt, leavening, and other dry ingredients are properly

distributed. If your baking powder or baking soda is not properly distributed, you may get air pockets and "tunnels" in your baked goods.

7. **Mix the ingredients in the order** and manner described in the recipe. How ingredients are mixed is as important as using the right amount of each ingredient. For example, did you know that if you add lemon juice to eggs before adding the sugar you'll "cook" the eggs?

8. **Avoid overworking the dough.** As soon as liquids are combined with flour, the protein in the flour (gluten) is activated. As you work the dough, the gluten gets stronger and the dough gets tougher. For tender biscuits and cakes, you won't want a tough dough, so mix only to combine ingredients. If you're making bread, on the other hand, you'll knead the dough to develop the gluten for that chewy texture.

9. **Follow resting and chilling times** specified in the recipe. Some doughs need to rest or chill before you work with them. If you roll pie dough as soon as it's made, without first resting it in the refrigerator, the butter will melt and gluten will develop. You'll end up with a tough piecrust with no flakiness.

10. **Use the specified size and type of baking pan.** These recipes are developed and tested for the size and type of pan specified. Using a different pan can change the baking time and outcome of a recipe. Try to use a pan as close to the size and shape as that listed in the recipe.

11. **Generally, bake in the middle rack of the oven,** unless otherwise specified in the recipe. If you've got hot spots in your oven (see page 5), flip and rotate your pans around to avoid burning your baked goods in those spots.

12. **Check for doneness before the minimum time.** Ambient temperature, pan materials, and oven fluctuations can all affect baking time. To be safe, I encourage you to begin checking your baked good several minutes before the recommended time.

13. **Let baked goods cool properly,** according to the recipe. Some baked goods, like my Jumbo Bread Pudding Muffins (page 23), are best eaten when slightly warm, but many others must cool completely before you eat them. If you slice a cake before it's cooled, for example, the starches won't have gelled, and the cake will fall apart.

IN A PINCH: EMERGENCY BAKING KIT

We've all had one of those moments: You're up to your elbows in flour before you realize that you don't have one of the key ingredients for the recipe. If you absolutely can't get to the grocery store, here are some common tricks for substituting or creating ingredients from what you probably already have in the pantry:

Baking powder For each teaspoon of baking powder, you can use ¼ teaspoon baking soda plus ½ teaspoon cream of tartar.

Brown sugar For each cup of brown sugar, use a cup of white sugar plus 1½ to 2 tablespoons molasses. Use less molasses to substitute light brown sugar and more to substitute dark brown sugar.

Buttermilk To replace a cup of buttermilk, stir 1 tablespoon lemon juice or white vinegar into a cup of whole milk. Set aside for 5 minutes to thicken. You can also use ¾ cup yogurt or sour cream thinned with ¼ cup milk or water.

Cake flour For each cup of cake flour, you can substitute ¾ cup all-purpose flour mixed with 2 tablespoons cornstarch.

Chocolate To replace an ounce of unsweetened chocolate, you can use 3 tablespoons cocoa powder plus 1 tablespoon butter or shortening. For semisweet chocolate, use 3 tablespoons cocoa powder plus 1 tablespoon butter or shortening plus 1 tablespoon sugar.

Sour cream Yogurt and sour cream are generally interchangeable. Greek yogurt is closest in texture to sour cream and is the best substitute.

THE RECIPES

This book will walk you through eight chapters of easy baking recipes. Each chapter covers a different baking category and will begin with a quick tutorial, including an overview, helpful hints, and a few shortcuts.

Once you're armed with that knowledge, we'll move into the recipes. There's no better way to start baking than by exploring muffins and quick breads—a great way to start an easy baking book (and not a bad way to start a day). Then we'll explore some sweet and other traditional baked treats: cookies and bars; cakes, cupcakes, and frostings; pies and tarts; and croissant and pastries.

In chapter 7, we'll dive into the magic or science—whatever you want to call it—of yeast breads. Finally, although savory foods may not be the first thing you equate with baking, there's an entire chapter devoted to favorite savory dishes from around the world. Oh, and to ensure that every member of the family gets represented, there's even a recipe for Peanut Butter Dog Biscuits (page 202).

Once these recipes become a part of your repertoire, you'll surely want to mix it up and experiment with different ingredients, variations, and add-ins.

Every recipe includes a tip of some sort, so as you go, you can learn how to save time, add variety, make ahead, substitute other ingredients, or gain technique insight. Before long, the term "easy baking" will evolve into "baking's easy!"

BACON & CORN MUFFINS *page 19*

Chapter 2

MUFFINS & QUICK BREADS

QUICK TUTORIAL

About Muffins & Quick Breads

A "muffin" is a specific baked good, but it's also the name of an easy mixing technique. To mix a batter with the "muffin method," you put all your dry ingredients together, put all your wet ingredients together, and then combine the two. Most quick breads are also mixed this way.

A quick bread is a loaf that doesn't contain yeast and isn't kneaded. It's also called tea bread. Quick bread batter is similar to muffin batter, so it's treated the same way. Muffin batter can often be baked as a quick bread, and vice versa.

Helpful Hints

◆ When you mix a batter using the muffin method, as soon as the dry and wet ingredients come together, two things happen: First, the gluten in the flour will start to develop, and second, the baking powder or baking soda will start forming carbon dioxide bubbles for leavening (rising). To avoid working the gluten too much or deflating the air bubbles, mix the batter just until the dry ingredients are absorbed.

Shortcuts/Time-Savers

◆ Since the texture of a muffin or quick bread is not as fine as the texture of a cake, there is no need to sift the dry ingredients. For these recipes, you can skip sifting and simply whisk together the dry ingredients. Whisking will sufficiently aerate and mix the ingredients.
◆ For muffins, you can butter and flour the muffin pan, or use paper cupcake liners. I like the rustic look of a muffin without a liner, but the liners do save time and cleanup.
◆ When baking quick breads in a loaf pan, first butter and flour the pan, then, if desired, line the pan with a parchment "sling." The sling makes getting the loaf out of the pan much easier and helps with cleanup. To make a sling, cut a piece of parchment paper 9 inches wide by 12 inches long. Line the pan so the paper hangs over either side.

GLAZED BLUEBERRY-LEMON MUFFINS

Makes 12 muffins

I'm willing to bet that if you asked someone to name one type of muffin, most people would say "blueberry." Blueberry is, arguably, the most popular muffin flavor. Blueberries are healthy and guilt-free, but they're also sweet enough to feel like a treat. With a sweet and tangy lemon glaze on top, these muffins really are a treat. NUT-FREE

PREP TIME: 10 minutes

BAKE TIME: 15 to 20 minutes

EQUIPMENT: 12-cup muffin pan, paper liners (optional), mixing bowls, whisk, rasp grater

2⅔ cups (14 ounces, 392g) all-purpose flour
½ cup (4 ounces, 112g) granulated sugar
1 tablespoon baking powder
1 teaspoon salt
2 large eggs
1 cup (8 ounces, 240 ml) whole milk
⅔ cup (5 ounces, 150 ml) vegetable oil
Finely grated zest of 1 large lemon
1½ cups (7 ounces, 200g) blueberries, fresh or frozen
3 tablespoons freshly squeezed lemon juice
1 cup (4 ounces, 112g) confectioners' sugar

1. Preheat the oven to 375°F. Butter and flour a 12-cup muffin pan or line with paper liners.

2. In a large mixing bowl, add the flour, granulated sugar, baking powder, and salt. Whisk together the dry ingredients.

3. In a separate bowl, whisk together the eggs, milk, oil, and lemon zest.

4. Make a well in the center of the dry ingredients and pour in the wet ingredients. Stir until the flour is barely incorporated, then gently fold in the blueberries. Scoop the batter into the prepared muffin pan.

5. Bake for 15 to 20 minutes, or until the center of a muffin springs back when lightly pressed or a toothpick inserted into the center of a muffin comes out with a few moist crumbs. While the muffins are baking, whisk together the lemon juice and confectioners' sugar until smooth.

Continued

6. Let the muffins cool in the pan for 10 minutes, until they're still warm but not too hot to handle. Lift each muffin out of the pan and dip the top into the lemon glaze. Allow the glaze to set for a few minutes before serving.

INGREDIENT TIP: If you are using frozen blueberries, don't thaw them before using. Thawed berries will leak juice and turn the batter green. This recipe makes 12 standard or six jumbo muffins. Jumbo muffins will need to cook a little longer—just use the same tests for doneness as directed in step 5.

BACON & CORN MUFFINS

Makes 12 muffins

These muffins are an entire breakfast in one neat little package. With savory bacon bits, crunchy cornmeal, and a little added sugar, this recipe rides the line between sweet and savory. For a heartier breakfast, you can bake the batter as 6 jumbo muffins instead of 12 standard muffins; they will just need to bake a little longer. NUT-FREE

PREP TIME: 10 minutes

BAKE TIME: 15 to 20 minutes

EQUIPMENT: Skillet, 12-cup muffin pan, paper liners (optional), mixing bowls, whisk

6 slices (8 ounces, 224g) thick-cut bacon

1 cup (5 ounces, 140g) yellow cornmeal, preferably stone-ground

1 cup (5 ounces, 140g) all-purpose flour

½ cup (4 ounces, 112g) granulated sugar

1 tablespoon baking powder

1 teaspoon salt

¾ cup (6 ounces, 180 ml) whole milk

2 large eggs

½ cup (3.5 ounces, 105 ml) vegetable oil or bacon fat

1. Preheat the oven to 375°F. Cook the bacon slices in a skillet until crisp, reserving the bacon fat. Chop the bacon into ½-inch bits and set aside. Grease a 12-cup muffin pan with the reserved bacon fat if desired, or line with paper liners.

2. In a large bowl, add the cornmeal, flour, sugar, baking powder, and salt. Whisk to combine.

3. In a separate bowl, whisk together the milk, eggs, and vegetable oil or bacon fat. If using the bacon fat, add enough oil to make ½ cup.

4. Make a well in the center of the dry ingredients and pour in the wet ingredients. Stir until the flour is barely incorporated, then fold in the bacon bits. Spoon the batter into the prepared muffin pan.

Continued

5. Bake for 15 to 20 minutes, until the center of a muffin springs back when lightly pressed or a toothpick inserted into the center of a muffin comes out with a few moist crumbs.

6. Let the muffins cool for 5 minutes before removing from the pan.

7. These are best eaten the day they are made, or you can wrap and freeze to enjoy later.

VARIATION TIP: You can leave out the bacon if you want to make vegetarian muffins.

BANANA STREUSEL MUFFINS

Makes 12 muffins

Bananas and walnuts are natural flavor partners. These muffins are made with layers of moist banana bread and crunchy brown sugar–walnut streusel. Brown sugar crumble topping is a perfectly sweet touch that makes the muffins extra special. This recipe makes 12 standard or 6 jumbo muffins—cook the jumbo muffins just a bit longer.

PREP TIME: 20 minutes

BAKE TIME: 15 to 20 minutes

EQUIPMENT: Food processor (optional), mixing bowls, electric mixer, spatula, 12-cup muffin pan, paper liners (optional)

FOR THE STREUSEL

¼ cup (2 ounces, 56g) packed brown sugar

¼ cup (2 ounces, 56g) granulated sugar

½ cup (2 ounces, 56g) walnuts

2 teaspoons ground cinnamon

¼ cup (1 ounce, 30g) cake flour

2 tablespoons (1 ounce, 30g) unsalted butter, at room temperature

FOR THE BATTER

1 large (6-ounce, 170g) peeled ripe banana

⅓ cup (3 ounces, 84g) sour cream

1 large egg

½ teaspoon vanilla extract

1½ cups (6 ounces, 170g) cake flour

½ cup (4 ounces, 112g) granulated sugar

½ teaspoon baking powder

¼ teaspoon baking soda

¼ teaspoon salt

1 stick (4 ounces, 112g) unsalted butter, at room temperature

TO MAKE THE STREUSEL

1. In a food processor, add the brown sugar, granulated sugar, walnuts, and cinnamon, and pulse until the nuts are chopped coarsely but not ground to a powder. Alternatively, finely chop the walnuts by hand, then toss them with the other ingredients in a mixing bowl. Set aside ⅓ cup of streusel for the filling.

2. Add the flour and butter to the remaining streusel and process or mix by hand until it begins to form clumps. Set aside.

TO MAKE THE MUFFINS

1. Preheat the oven to 375°F. Butter and flour a 12-cup muffin pan or line with paper liners.

2. In a small bowl, smash the banana with the back of a fork until you have a chunky purée. Mix in the sour cream, egg, and vanilla. Set aside.

Continued

3. In a separate bowl, add the flour, sugar, baking powder, baking soda, and salt. Mix the dry ingredients with an electric mixer on low speed. Add the butter and half of the banana mixture. Increase the speed to medium and mix for 2 to 3 minutes to lighten the batter. Use a spatula to scrape down the side of the bowl. Add the remaining banana mixture and mix until blended.

4. Spoon a few tablespoons of batter into each of the prepared muffin cups, filling no more than one-third full. Sprinkle a teaspoon of streusel over each muffin. Dollop the remaining batter over the streusel and gently smooth into an even layer. Break big clumps of streusel topping into smaller chunks over the muffins, dividing the topping evenly among the muffins.

5. Bake for 15 to 20 minutes, or until the center of a muffin in the middle of the pan springs back when lightly touched or a toothpick inserted in the center comes out with a few moist crumbs. Let the muffins cool for 10 minutes before removing from the pan.

INGREDIENT TIP: When I bake with bananas, I prefer to mash them with a fork, rather than purée them in a blender or food processor. I like to have some chunks of banana visible, and I find that puréed bananas can become gummy.

JUMBO BREAD PUDDING MUFFINS

Makes 6 muffins

Bread pudding is pure comfort food; it's the fuzzy slippers of baked goods. With this recipe we turn traditional bread pudding into jumbo muffins, which can be served for breakfast, brunch, or dessert. The dried cranberries and apples add moisture and a wonderful bright note, which balances perfectly with the rich custard and warm spices. NUT-FREE

PREP TIME: 30 minutes

BAKE TIME: 15 minutes

EQUIPMENT: Mixing bowls, grater (optional), 6-cup muffin pan, container with spout, whisk

1 cup (5 ounces, 140g) dried cranberries

1 large apple, peeled and minced or grated on the large holes of a grater

¼ cup (2 ounces, 60 ml) dark rum or apple juice

1 teaspoon vanilla extract

½ cup (4 ounces, 112g) granulated sugar, plus more for the pan

6 cups (6 ounces, 180g) cubed day-old bread

1 teaspoon ground cinnamon

¼ teaspoon ground nutmeg

¼ teaspoon ground ginger

2 cups (16 ounces, 473 ml) whole milk

4 large eggs

Demerara or granulated sugar, for sprinkling

1. In a bowl, toss together the cranberries, grated apple, rum, and vanilla. Set aside for at least 30 minutes to meld the flavors.

2. Preheat the oven to 325°F. Butter a 6-cup jumbo muffin pan and sprinkle granulated sugar into the pan and swirl the pan to coat the inside of the cups with the sugar.

3. In a large bowl, toss the bread cubes with the cinnamon, nutmeg, and ginger. Add the cranberry-apple mixture to the bread cubes, stirring to evenly distribute the fruit. Divide the bread cube mixture evenly among the muffin cups.

4. In a container with a pouring spout, make a custard by whisking together the milk, eggs, and ½ cup of granulated sugar. Pour the custard over the bread cubes, dividing it evenly among the muffin cups. Set aside for 10 minutes to allow the bread to absorb the custard.

Continued

5. Sprinkle Demerara or granulated sugar evenly over the surface of each muffin and bake until the custard is set, about 15 minutes. Serve warm.

VARIATION TIP: Switch out the cranberries for another dried fruit, swap the apples for another fresh fruit, and change the mix of spices to create any version of bread pudding that you'd like. This recipe can also be baked in an 8-inch-square pan. Leftovers can be refrigerated for several days or frozen for up to 3 months.

RAISIN SCONES

Makes 24 scones

I guarantee that this is an authentic scone recipe. I made it when I worked in a British tea shop, where my raisin scones got the personal approval of the owner's British mom. A traditional scone should not have the texture of a biscuit nor that of a muffin; rather, it should be somewhere between the two. Scones are delicious served with butter and maybe a dollop of jam. If you want to put on a formal afternoon tea, the traditional way to serve scones is with clotted cream, jam, and lemon curd (see Tip). NUT-FREE

PREP TIME: 20 minutes

BAKE TIME: 15 to 20 minutes

EQUIPMENT: Baking sheets, parchment paper or silicone baking mats, mixing bowls, whisk, spatula or wooden spoon, biscuit cutter (optional)

2 large eggs

1¾ cups (14 ounces, 420 ml) buttermilk, plus more for brushing

5 cups (25 ounces, 700g) all-purpose flour

½ cup (4 ounces, 112g) granulated sugar

2 tablespoons baking powder

½ teaspoon salt

1½ sticks (6 ounces, 168g) cold unsalted butter, cut into 1-inch chunks

¾ cup (6 ounces, 168g) raisins

Demerara or granulated sugar, for sprinkling

1. Preheat the oven to 400°F. Line two baking sheets with parchment paper or silicone baking mats.

2. In a small bowl, whisk together the eggs and buttermilk. Set aside.

3. In a large bowl, whisk together the flour, granulated sugar, baking powder, and salt.

4. Using your fingers, work the butter into the dry ingredients until the bits of butter are no larger than pea-size.

5. Add the buttermilk mixture all at once and mix with a spatula or wooden spoon until barely incorporated, being careful not to overmix. Some loose flour will remain at the bottom of the bowl. Transfer the dough onto a floured surface. Sprinkle the raisins over the dough and finish kneading by hand until the loose flour is absorbed. This should take 15 to 20 turns. Use your hands to pat the dough until it is 1 inch thick.

Continued

6. Use a 2.5-inch biscuit cutter or the rim of a drinking glass to cut the scones. Gently re-roll the scraps and continue cutting until all the dough is used. Transfer the scones to the prepared baking sheets. Brush the tops with buttermilk and sprinkle with Demerara or granulated sugar.

7. Bake the scones on the middle rack of the oven for 15 to 20 minutes, rotating the baking sheets after 10 minutes. The scones are ready when they are golden brown and sound hollow when the bottom is tapped.

INGREDIENT TIP: Demerara sugar is a coarsely granulated brown sugar with large crystals that leave a nice finish. It's available in most markets or online, but granulated sugar is a fine substitute. The raisins are traditional, but if you'd prefer not to use them, you can leave them out or use any other chopped dried fruit instead. And if the idea of a traditional tea appeals to you, clotted cream can be bought online or in some larger markets. Mascarpone cheese is a good substitute for clotted cream. Lemon curd is available in the jam aisle of many markets or online.

SUGAR & SPICE SCONES

Makes 8 scones

Raisin Scones (page 25), topped with butter and jam or clotted cream, jam, and lemon curd, are traditional for afternoon tea. These Sugar & Spice Scones are a little sweeter and lighter than the raisin ones, and they don't need any topping. This dough comes together in mere minutes and bakes in under 30. Yes, less than an hour after rolling out of bed, you can have warm scones for breakfast. NUT-FREE

PREP TIME: 10 minutes
BAKE TIME: About 25 minutes
EQUIPMENT: Baking sheet, parchment paper or silicone baking mats, mixing bowls, whisk, pastry brush

1 egg
½ teaspoon salt, plus pinch
2 cups (10 ounces, 285g)
    all-purpose flour
¾ cup (6 ounces, 168g) granulated sugar
1 tablespoon baking powder
½ teaspoon ground cinnamon
¼ teaspoon ground ginger
¼ teaspoon ground cloves
¼ teaspoon ground nutmeg
¼ teaspoon ground cardamom
1 stick (4 ounces, 112g) unsalted butter,
    at room temperature
1 cup (8 ounces, 240 ml) whole milk
Demerara or granulated sugar, for
    sprinkling

1. Preheat the oven to 375°F. Line a baking sheet with parchment paper or a silicone baking mat.

2. In a small bowl, whisk the egg with a pinch of salt. Set aside.

3. In a mixing bowl, whisk together the flour, granulated sugar, baking powder, the remaining ½ teaspoon of salt, cinnamon, ginger, cloves, nutmeg, and cardamom. Use your fingers to work the butter into the dry ingredients until the bits are no larger than pea-size.

4. Add the milk all at once and mix just until the flour is absorbed. Transfer the dough directly to the baking sheet and, using well-floured hands, pat it into an 8-inch round. Use a sharp knife to lightly score the round into 8 wedges. Brush the top with the egg wash and sprinkle with Demerara or granulated sugar.

Continued

SUGAR & SPICE SCONES *Continued*

5. Bake for about 25 minutes, or until golden brown and a toothpick inserted in the center comes out clean. Let cool for 15 minutes, then use a serrated knife to fully cut into wedges.

MAKE-AHEAD TIP: Mix the dry ingredients and cut in the butter the night before. Cover and set aside at room temperature. In the morning, while you preheat the oven, you can add the milk and finish mixing the dough.

HONEY-PUMPKIN BREAD

Makes 16 slices

Pumpkin bread is such a great snack. This one is lightly sweet
and moist, and has just enough spice to highlight the pumpkin
flavor without overpowering it. No need to wait for autumn
to enjoy this bread. It's good enough to eat year-round.
This batter can also be baked in muffin tins. NUT-FREE

PREP TIME: 15 minutes

BAKE TIME: 1 hour

EQUIPMENT: 9-by-5-inch loaf pan,
parchment paper (optional), mixing
bowls, whisk

1⅔ cups (9 ounces, 255g)
    all-purpose flour
⅔ cup (6 ounces, 170g) granulated
    sugar, plus 2 tablespoons
1 teaspoon ground cinnamon
½ teaspoon ground nutmeg
½ teaspoon ground cloves
¾ teaspoon baking soda
¼ teaspoon salt
3 large eggs
⅔ cup (5 ounces, 150 ml) vegetable oil
⅓ cup (4 ounces, 112g) honey
½ teaspoon lemon extract
2 teaspoons vanilla extract
1 cup (8 ounces, 230g) canned
    pumpkin purée

1. Preheat the oven to 350°F. Butter and
flour a 9-by-5-inch loaf pan, or butter the
pan and line with parchment paper.

2. In a large bowl, whisk together the flour,
⅔ cup of sugar, cinnamon, nutmeg, cloves,
baking soda, and salt. Set aside.

3. In another bowl, mix the eggs, oil, honey,
lemon extract, vanilla, and pumpkin purée
until well combined. Make a well in the
middle of the dry ingredients and add
the wet ingredients. Mix until the flour is
incorporated.

4. Pour the batter into the prepared pan
and spread to level. Sprinkle the remaining
2 tablespoons of sugar over the surface of
the batter.

5. Bake for about 1 hour, or until a toothpick
inserted in the center comes out with a few
moist crumbs. Let cool in the pan for 10 minutes, then turn out onto a cooling rack. Let
cool to room temperature before slicing.

INGREDIENT TIP: Make sure you use
pure pumpkin purée, not pumpkin pie mix.
Pumpkin pie mix has added sugar, water,
spices, and "other flavors." Canned pumpkin is just pure pumpkin—that's what you
want for this recipe.

CHOCOLATE CHIP BANANA BREAD

⟩ Makes 12 slices ⟨

Slightly overripe bananas are best for baking. As bananas ripen the starches turn to sugar, and they become softer and sweeter. For baking, bananas should be well-speckled, but not black and mushy. A hint of cinnamon and nutmeg, along with a splash of lemon extract, brings out the banana flavor in this bread. The chocolate chips are a bonus. If you like nuts, a cup of chopped walnuts is another nice addition to this bread. NUT-FREE

PREP TIME: 15 minutes

BAKE TIME: 1 hour 5 minutes

EQUIPMENT: 9-by-5-inch loaf pan, parchment paper (optional), mixing bowls, whisk

3 or 4 fully ripe medium bananas (12 ounces, 340g)

⅓ cup (3 ounces, 84g) full-fat Greek yogurt or sour cream

¼ cup (1.75 ounces, 52.5 ml) vegetable oil

2 large eggs

1 teaspoon vanilla extract

½ teaspoon lemon extract

1 cup (6 ounces, 170g) mini chocolate chips, plus more for sprinkling (optional)

2 cups (10 ounces, 283g) all-purpose flour, plus 1 teaspoon

½ cup (4 ounces, 112g) granulated sugar

¼ cup (2 ounces, 56g) packed brown sugar

1 teaspoon baking powder

½ teaspoon baking soda

½ teaspoon salt

½ teaspoon ground cinnamon

¼ teaspoon ground nutmeg

1. Preheat the oven to 350°F. Butter and flour a 9-by-5-inch loaf pan, or butter the pan and line with parchment paper.

2. In a bowl, mash the bananas with a fork, leaving them a little chunky. Add the yogurt, oil, eggs, vanilla, and lemon extract to the bananas. Mix together and set aside. In another bowl, toss the chocolate chips with 2 teaspoons of water to moisten (see Tip). Sprinkle 1 teaspoon of flour over the chips and toss. Set aside.

3. In a large bowl, whisk together the remaining 2 cups of flour, granulated sugar, brown sugar, baking powder, baking soda, salt, cinnamon, and nutmeg. Make a well in the center. Add the banana mixture and stir until about two-thirds of the flour is incorporated. Fold in the chocolate chips and mix until all the flour is incorporated.

4. Pour the batter into the prepared pan and spread to level. Sprinkle additional chocolate chips on top if desired.

5. Bake for about 1 hour and 5 minutes, or until golden brown and a toothpick inserted in the middle comes out with a few moist crumbs.

6. Let the bread cool for 10 minutes in the pan, then turn out onto a cooling rack to cool completely before slicing.

TECHNIQUE TIP: Tossing the chocolate chips with flour and water creates a paste on the chips that helps keep them suspended in the batter while the bread bakes. Also, the parchment only lines the pan in one direction, so buttering the pan keeps the bread from sticking to the unlined parts of the pan, especially the corners. The butter also helps keep the parchment in place, which makes it a little easier to fill the pan with the batter.

ZUCCHINI BREAD

Makes 12 slices

Baking with veggies is especially satisfying because you feel like
you're being a little bit healthy. This recipe is not shy with the zucchini,
with a full pound in one loaf. This is great news if you are a gardener,
as zucchini is notoriously prolific. Even if you don't grow your own,
zucchini is inexpensive and available year-round in most markets.
This bread freezes beautifully, so you can stock the freezer in summer
and enjoy zucchini bread all winter long. DAIRY-FREE, NUT-FREE

- -

PREP TIME: 15 minutes

BAKE TIME: 45 to 50 minutes

EQUIPMENT: 9-by-5-inch loaf pan,
parchment paper (optional), grater,
mixing bowls, whisk

2 medium (16 ounces, 454g) zucchini

1 cup (8 ounces, 224g) packed
    brown sugar

¼ cup (1.75 ounces, 52.5 ml) vegetable oil

2 large eggs

2 cups (10 ounces, 285g)
    all-purpose flour

1 teaspoon ground cinnamon

½ teaspoon ground ginger

¼ teaspoon ground nutmeg

½ teaspoon salt

1½ teaspoons baking powder

¼ teaspoon baking soda

1. Preheat the oven to 350°F. Butter and
flour a 9-by-5-inch loaf pan, or butter and
line with parchment paper.

2. Use the large holes of a grater to shred
the zucchini. On a paper towel, spread the
shredded zucchini in an even layer and
cover with another paper towel. Press to
absorb the liquid. Let the zucchini sit while
you mix the batter.

3. In a medium bowl, whisk together the
brown sugar, oil, and eggs. Fold in the
zucchini.

4. In a separate bowl, whisk together the
flour, cinnamon, ginger, nutmeg, salt, baking powder, and baking soda. Add the wet
ingredients to the dry ingredients and stir
until incorporated.

5. Pour the batter into the prepared loaf pan. Bake for 45 to 50 minutes, until a toothpick inserted into the center of the loaf comes out with a few moist crumbs.

6. Let cool in the pan for 20 minutes, then turn out onto a cooling rack to cool completely before slicing.

VARIATION TIP: To make chocolate zucchini bread, replace ½ cup of the flour with an equal amount of cocoa powder. To gild the lily, you can fold in a cup of mini chocolate chips. To make whole-wheat zucchini bread, replace ½ cup of the all-purpose flour with ½ cup of whole-wheat flour.

APPLESAUCE LOAF

Makes 12 slices

Because of the applesauce in the batter, this loaf is very tender and has a pleasantly sweet taste. Applesauce contains carbohydrates and fiber, which work the same way fat does in a recipe. By replacing some of the oil in this recipe with applesauce, we make a treat that is lower in fat but still soft and moist. It's a wonderful breakfast treat or afternoon snack. DAIRY-FREE, NUT-FREE

PREP TIME: 10 minutes

BAKE TIME: 55 to 60 minutes

EQUIPMENT: 9-by-5-inch loaf pan, parchment paper (optional), mixing bowls, whisk

½ cup (3.5 ounces, 105 ml) vegetable oil

¾ cup (6 ounces, 168g) applesauce

½ cup (4 ounces, 112g) granulated sugar

½ cup (4 ounces, 112g) packed brown sugar

2 large eggs

1½ teaspoons vanilla extract

1½ cups (7.5 ounces, 210g) all-purpose flour

½ teaspoon baking powder

¼ teaspoon baking soda

2 teaspoons ground cinnamon

½ teaspoon ground ginger

¼ teaspoon ground nutmeg

½ teaspoon salt

½ cup (1.8 ounces, 50g) rolled oats

1. Preheat the oven to 350°F. Butter and flour a 9-by-5-inch loaf pan, or butter the pan and line with parchment paper.

2. In a small bowl, mix together the oil, applesauce, granulated sugar, brown sugar, eggs, and vanilla. Set aside.

3. In a separate bowl, whisk together the flour, baking powder, baking soda, cinnamon, ginger, nutmeg, and salt. Whisk to combine the ingredients, then mix in the rolled oats. Make a well in the center of the dry ingredients and pour in the wet ingredients. Mix to combine.

4. Pour the batter into the prepared pan. Bake for 55 to 60 minutes, or until golden brown and a toothpick inserted in the center comes out with a few moist crumbs. Let cool completely before slicing.

STORAGE TIP: The loaf can be stored, well-wrapped, at room temperature for several days. For longer storage, the loaf can be double-wrapped and frozen for up to 3 months.

IRISH SODA BREAD

> *Makes 16 slices*

Even if you're reluctant to make your own bread, soda bread is so easy, it's worth giving a try. There's no yeast or fussy fermentation, no rolling or cutting. In fact, soda bread is even easier to make than muffins or biscuits. You don't even have to use an electric mixer. Mixing by hand helps ensure that you won't overwork and toughen the dough, and it comes together in mere minutes. NUT-FREE

PREP TIME: 15 minutes

BAKE TIME: 50 to 55 minutes

EQUIPMENT: Baking sheet, parchment paper or silicone baking mat, mixing bowls, whisk

4 cups (20 ounces, 570g) all-purpose flour

2 tablespoons (1 ounce, 30g) granulated sugar

1 teaspoon salt

1½ teaspoons baking powder

½ teaspoon baking soda

3 tablespoons (1.5 ounces, 45g) butter, at room temperature

1 cup (6 ounces, 170g) raisins

2 cups (16 ounces, 500 ml) buttermilk, plus more for brushing

CLEANUP TIP: If your hands get coated with the sticky dough, don't try to wash it off with water—it'll just get stickier and leave a mess in the sink. Dip your hands in the flour bin to coat them. Over a trash can, rub your hands together vigorously, and the sticky dough will come off easily.

1. Preheat the oven to 375°F. Line a baking sheet with parchment paper or a silicone baking mat.

2. In a large bowl, whisk together the flour, sugar, salt, baking powder, and baking soda. Using your fingers, work the butter into the dry ingredients until the pieces are no larger than pea-size. Toss the raisins in with the dry ingredients.

3. Add the buttermilk all at once and mix until the dry ingredients are almost incorporated. The dough will be dry at this point, but will come together. Turn the dough onto a floured surface and knead 15 to 20 times to form a smooth ball.

4. Place the loaf onto the prepared baking sheet. Use your hands to flatten the ball slightly, then use a sharp knife to cut a ¾-inch-deep X into the top of the loaf. Brush the loaf with more buttermilk.

5. Bake for 50 to 55 minutes, or until the loaf is golden brown and sounds hollow when tapped on the bottom.

6. Let the soda bread cool to room temperature before slicing. Pick any burnt raisins off the surface of the bread before serving, if desired.

TRUE STRAWBERRY SHORTCAKES

Makes 12 shortcakes

Shortcakes are one of my favorite summertime desserts, especially for casual get-togethers. You can prepare all the components, then let your guests build their own dessert. These shortcakes are similar to my Flaky Buttermilk Biscuits (page 201), but the addition of a few eggs and some sugar makes them a little lighter and more cake-like than a plain biscuit. That lighter texture is perfect for absorbing the delicious strawberry juices. You can make this same recipe with whatever fruit is in season. Peach shortcakes are fantastic later in the summer. NUT-FREE

PREP TIME: 30 minutes

BAKE TIME: 12 to 14 minutes

EQUIPMENT: Baking sheet, parchment paper or silicone baking mat, mixing bowls, whisk, biscuit cutter (optional)

FOR THE SHORTCAKES

2 cups (10 ounces, 285g) all-purpose flour

2 cups (9 ounces, 260g) cake flour

¼ cup (2 ounces, 55g) granulated sugar, plus more for sprinkling

2 tablespoons baking powder

1 teaspoon salt

2 sticks (8 ounces, 224g) cold unsalted butter, cut into ¼-inch slices

2 large eggs

1½ cups (12 ounces, 360 ml) buttermilk, plus more for brushing

FOR THE FILLING

1½ pounds ripe strawberries, stems removed

¾ cup (6 ounces, 168g) granulated sugar, divided

2 cups (1 pint, 473 ml) heavy cream

1 tablespoon vanilla extract

TO MAKE THE SHORTCAKES

1. Preheat the oven to 375°F. Line a baking sheet with parchment paper or a silicone baking mat.

2. In a large bowl, whisk together the all-purpose flour, cake flour, sugar, baking powder, and salt. Add the butter slices. Using your fingers, work the butter into the flour until the pieces are no larger than pea-size.

3. Whisk together the eggs and buttermilk and pour the mixture into the dry ingredients. Mix with a spoon or spatula until a dough begins to form. With well-floured hands, turn the wet dough out onto a well-floured surface and knead 10 to 15 times to bring it together.

4. Use your hands to pat the dough down to ¾ inch thick. Cut out rounds with a 2½- or 3-inch biscuit cutter or the rim of a glass. Pat the scraps together and continue cutting out rounds until you have a total of 12 shortcakes.

5. Place the rounds on the prepared baking pan. Brush the tops with buttermilk and sprinkle with sugar. Bake for 12 to 14 minutes, or until golden brown. Let cool before assembling.

TO MAKE THE FILLING

1. Slice the berries and place them in a large bowl. Fold in ½ cup of sugar and set aside for at least 30 minutes.

2. Whip the cream with the remaining ¼ cup of sugar and the vanilla until soft peaks form.

3. Split the shortcakes and top with berries and cream.

MAKE-AHEAD TIP: Bake the shortcakes and freeze them for up to 1 month. Let thaw, then warm them in a 350°F oven for 5 minutes. This will revive the texture. Fill and serve the shortcakes as directed.

LEMON BARS *page 67*

Chapter 3

COOKIES & BARS

QUICK TUTORIAL

About Cookies & Bars

There are four basic types of cookies, and all the recipes in this chapter fall into one of these categories.

- **Drop cookies** are made with a soft dough that is scooped and "dropped" onto the baking sheet. Because the dough is soft, these cookies usually spread as they bake.
- **Cutout cookies** are made with a slightly firmer dough, which is rolled and cut into specific shapes by hand or with a cookie cutter.
- **Refrigerator cookies** are rolled into logs and chilled, then sliced and baked.
- **Bar cookies,** such as brownies, blondies, and lemon bars, are made from a soft batter or dough. The batter or dough is baked in a cake pan, then cut into individual bars.

Helpful Hints

- Scooped cookie dough can be refrigerated or frozen to bake later. When you make cookie dough, make extra and freeze so you can quickly bake up fresh cookies anytime the mood strikes.
- For rolled and sliced cookies, it's easiest to work with dough that has been chilled long enough to firm it up, but not so long that the dough is too stiff to work with.
- When making bar cookies, life is much easier if you line the pan with parchment paper to help lift the uncut cookies out after baking.

Shortcuts/Time-Savers

- The number-one time-saver when baking cookies is to use parchment paper or a silicone baking mat to line the baking sheet. Parchment paper makes it easy to slide the cookies off the baking sheet; it also prevents the cookies from spreading too much, so cleanup is much easier.
- Even without parchment paper or a silicone baking mat, you don't need to grease the baking sheet. Most cookie doughs have enough fat in them to prevent the cookies from sticking. In fact, if you butter the baking sheet, the cookies may spread too much.
- When making drop cookies, an inexpensive cookie scoop is a great time-saver. This simple tool makes quick work of portioning cookies. Plus, scooped cookies are a consistent size, so they'll bake more evenly.

OATMEAL-MAPLE COOKIES

Makes 24 cookies

This is my family's all-time favorite cookie recipe. We've dubbed them "Magic Oatmeal Cookies" because almost every time I serve them, someone says, "These are the best cookies I've ever tasted." The real maple syrup in the glaze makes the cookies extra tasty. NUT-FREE

PREP TIME: 15 minutes
BAKE TIME: 8 to 10 minutes
EQUIPMENT: Baking sheets, parchment paper or silicone baking mats, mesh sieve or sifter, mixing bowls, electric mixer, cookie scoop (optional)

FOR THE COOKIES

¾ cup (3.75 ounces, 105g)
    all-purpose flour
½ teaspoon ground cinnamon
½ teaspoon baking soda
¼ teaspoon salt
1 stick (4 ounces, 112g) unsalted butter,
    at room temperature
½ cup (4 ounces, 112g) packed
    brown sugar
¼ cup (2 ounces, 56g) granulated sugar
1 large egg
½ teaspoon vanilla extract
1½ cups (5 ounces, 135g) old-fashioned
    rolled oats

FOR THE MAPLE GLAZE

1 cup (4 ounces, 112g)
    confectioners' sugar
¼ cup (2 ounces, 60 ml) pure
    maple syrup

TO MAKE THE COOKIES

1. Preheat the oven to 350°F. Line two baking sheets with parchment paper or silicone baking mats.

2. Sift the flour, cinnamon, baking soda, and salt into a small bowl and set aside.

3. In a large bowl, using an electric mixer, cream the butter with the brown sugar and granulated sugar on medium speed until the mixture lightens in color and becomes fluffy. Scrape the bowl and the beaters. Add the egg and vanilla, and mix just until combined.

4. With the mixer running on low speed, add the flour mixture and mix until almost combined. Add the oats and mix to combine.

5. Use a cookie scoop or tablespoon to portion the dough into 1½-inch balls. Line the cookies 2 inches apart on the prepared baking sheets. Bake for 8 to 10 minutes, or until the cookies are golden brown around the edges and the centers are just barely set.

6. Let the cookies cool on the baking sheets until slightly warm and you can pick them up without breaking.

Continued

OATMEAL-MAPLE COOKIES *Continued*

TO MAKE THE MAPLE GLAZE

1. In a small bowl, add the confectioners' sugar and maple syrup. Stir until the glaze is smooth.

2. Spread the glaze on the cookies while they're still slightly warm. The glaze will set while the cookies finish cooling.

MAKE-AHEAD TIP: Portioned cookie dough can be frozen on a baking sheet and then packed into freezer bags. No need to thaw before baking. The dough balls can go straight from the freezer into a preheated oven. Leftover glaze can be refrigerated for a couple of weeks and used as you bake the cookies. The cookies will keep several days in an airtight container at room temperature.

CHOCOLATE CHIP COOKIES

Makes 24 cookies

The chocolate chip cookie is the quintessential all-American cookie. Most recipes for this cookie are similar, made with a mix of white and brown sugar and lots of chocolate chips. I like to use mini chips for better distribution of the chocolate in the cookies, but you can use regular-size chips or chocolate chunks if you prefer. NUT-FREE

PREP TIME: 15 minutes

BAKE TIME: 8 to 10 minutes

EQUIPMENT: Baking sheets, parchment paper or silicone baking mats, mesh sieve or sifter, mixing bowls, electric mixer, cookie scoop (optional)

1¼ cups (6.25 ounces, 177g) all-purpose flour

½ teaspoon baking soda

¼ teaspoon salt

1 stick (4 ounces, 112g) unsalted butter, at room temperature

½ cup (4 ounces, 112g) packed dark brown sugar

¼ cup (2 ounces, 56g) granulated sugar

1 large egg

1 teaspoon vanilla extract

1 cup (6 ounces, 170g) mini chocolate chips

TECHNIQUE TIP: The key to a good chocolate chip cookie? Make sure the butter is not too soft when you mix the dough. If the butter is very soft, the cookies will spread more and be thinner. If you have time, chill the dough in the refrigerator for a couple of hours before baking. The cookies also do very well if the dough balls are frozen and then baked.

1. Preheat the oven to 350°F. Line two baking sheets with parchment paper or silicone baking mats.

2. Sift the flour, baking soda, and salt into a small bowl and set aside.

3. In a large bowl, using an electric mixer, cream the butter with the brown sugar and granulated sugar on medium speed until the mixture lightens in color and becomes aerated. Scrape the bowl and the beaters. Add the egg and vanilla, and mix just until combined.

4. With the mixer running on low speed, add the flour mixture and mix until almost combined. Fold in the chocolate chips by hand.

5. Use a cookie scoop or tablespoon to portion the dough into 1½-inch balls. Line the cookies 2 inches apart on the prepared baking sheets. Bake for 8 to 10 minutes, or until the cookies are golden brown around the edges and the centers are barely set. Let cool on a wire rack until firm enough to pick up without breaking.

SNICKERDOODLES

Makes 44 cookies

Snickerdoodles are wonderful, old-fashioned cinnamon-coated cookies. This dough is a little unusual because you must use cream of tartar and baking soda instead of baking powder. Don't be tempted to skip the cream of tartar, since that's what gives snickerdoodles their special flavor and texture. NUT-FREE

PREP TIME: 20 minutes

BAKE TIME: 10 to 12 minutes

EQUIPMENT: Baking sheets, parchment paper or silicone baking mats, whisk, mixing bowls, electric mixer, cookie scoop (optional)

1¾ cups (14 ounces, 392g) granulated sugar, divided
1 tablespoon ground cinnamon
3 cups (15 ounces, 420g) all-purpose flour
1½ teaspoons cream of tartar
1 teaspoon baking soda
¼ teaspoon salt
2 sticks (8 ounces, 224g) unsalted butter, at room temperature
2 large eggs, at room temperature

INGREDIENT TIP: Cream of tartar is an acidic powder that is a by-product of wine-making. It gives snickerdoodles a slightly acidic flavor and interferes with sugar crystallization. This is what makes these cookies soft and chewy, instead of crisp and crunchy like sugar cookies.

1. Preheat the oven to 375°F. Line two baking sheets with parchment paper or silicone baking mats.

2. In a pie plate or other wide, flat bowl, combine ¼ cup of sugar with the cinnamon. Set aside.

3. In a medium bowl, whisk together the flour, cream of tartar, baking soda, and salt. Set aside.

4. In a large bowl, using an electric mixer, cream the butter with the remaining 1½ cups of sugar until light and airy. Add the eggs, one at a time. Add the flour mixture and mix just until incorporated.

5. Use a cookie scoop or tablespoon to portion the dough into 1½-inch balls. Roll each ball in the cinnamon-sugar mixture and line them 2 inches apart on the prepared baking sheets.

6. Bake for 10 to 12 minutes, or until the cookies are slightly puffed and crackled on top, but still soft. Transfer to a wire rack to cool completely.

ESPRESSO TOFFEE CHUNK COOKIES

Makes 48 cookies

These cookies are thin, crisp, and loaded with crunchy toffee bits. With plenty of espresso flavor, these are a treat for grown-ups. I created this recipe to mimic the flavor of my all-time-favorite ice cream. Beware: These cookies are addictive! NUT-FREE

PREP TIME: 10 minutes

BAKE TIME: 10 minutes

EQUIPMENT: Baking sheets, parchment paper or silicone baking mats, whisk, mixing bowls, electric mixer, cookie scoop (optional)

2¼ cups (11.5 ounces, 330g) all-purpose flour

2 tablespoons (1 ounce, 20g) cocoa powder

1 teaspoon salt

1 teaspoon baking soda

2 sticks (8 ounces, 224g) unsalted butter, at room temperature

½ cup (4 ounces, 112g) granulated sugar

1 cup (8 ounces, 224g) packed brown sugar

¼ cup (2.25 ounces, 65g) instant espresso powder

1 tablespoon vanilla extract

2 eggs

2 cups (13 ounces, 370g) chocolate toffee chunks

INGREDIENT TIP: Make sure to use instant espresso powder, not ground espresso beans. Espresso powder will melt into the dough, but ground espresso beans will not.

1. Preheat the oven to 350°F. Line two baking sheets with parchment paper or silicone baking mats.

2. In a bowl, whisk together the flour, cocoa, salt, and baking soda. Set aside.

3. In a large bowl, using an electric mixer, cream the butter with the granulated sugar, brown sugar, espresso powder, and vanilla until light and fluffy.

4. Add the eggs to the butter-sugar mixture and mix until incorporated. Add the dry ingredients and mix until incorporated.

5. Gently fold in the toffee chunks by hand.

6. Use a cookie scoop or tablespoon to form 48 dough balls, and line them 2 inches apart on the prepared baking sheets. Alternatively, the cookie balls can be frozen and stored for up to a month before baking.

7. Bake the cookies for about 10 minutes, or until barely set in the middle. Let cool on the baking sheets for 5 minutes, then transfer to a wire rack to cool completely.

COCONUT MACAROONS

Makes 24 cookies

You only need 10 minutes and four ingredients to make these macaroons. They are so quick to make, you can have the batter ready before the oven is preheated. The cookies bake up light and chewy, and they keep for days in a cookie jar or covered container. DAIRY-FREE, GLUTEN-FREE, NUT-FREE

PREP TIME: 10 minutes

BAKE TIME: 20 minutes

EQUIPMENT: Baking sheets, parchment paper or silicone baking mats, mixing bowls, electric mixer, cookie scoop (optional)

3 egg whites

¼ cup plus 2 tablespoons (3 ounces, 85g) granulated sugar

1 teaspoon vanilla extract

1 (14-ounce) bag sweetened coconut flakes

VARIATION TIP: Fold in ½ cup of mini chocolate chips to make Chocolate Chip Macaroons. To make Almond Joy Macaroons, fold in ½ cup of chopped toasted almonds and dip the bottoms of the baked macaroons in melted chocolate.

1. Preheat the oven to 350°F. Line a baking sheet with parchment paper or a silicone baking mat.

2. In a large bowl, using an electric mixer, whisk the egg whites until soft peaks form. Slowly add the sugar and whip to full peaks. Add the vanilla.

3. Fold the coconut into the egg white mixture, breaking up any clumps.

4. Use a cookie scoop or tablespoon to portion the dough into 1½-inch mounds. Line the cookies 1 inch apart on the prepared baking sheet.

5. Bake for 10 minutes, then slide a second baking sheet directly under the cookies to keep the bottoms from over-browning.

6. Bake for another 10 minutes, or until the cookies are lightly golden brown and bounce back when you squeeze gently.

7. Transfer the parchment with the cookies to a wire rack and let cool completely.

MEXICAN WEDDING COOKIES

Makes 36 cookies

This cookie recipe has many names. I call them Mexican Wedding Cookies, but they're also known as Russian Tea Cookies, Italian Wedding Cookies, Butterballs, and Snowballs. The same dough can be made with walnuts instead of pecans and formed into crescents to make Walnut Crescent Cookies. Whatever you call them, these cookies are delicious and very pretty.

PREP TIME: 15 minutes, plus 30 minutes resting time
BAKE TIME: 18 to 20 minutes
EQUIPMENT: Nonstick frying pan, baking sheets, parchment paper or silicone baking mats, food processor, mixing bowls, cookie scoop (optional)

2 cups (7 ounces, 200g) pecans
½ cup (4 ounces, 112g) granulated sugar
¾ teaspoon salt
½ teaspoon ground cinnamon
1½ teaspoons vanilla extract
2 sticks (8 ounces, 224g) unsalted butter, at room temperature
2 cups (10 ounces, 280g) all-purpose flour
1½ cups (6 ounces, 170g) confectioners' sugar

1. In a large nonstick frying pan over medium-high heat, toast the pecans for 3 to 4 minutes, shaking the pan constantly so the nuts don't burn. They will become fragrant and lightly toasted. Set aside to cool completely.

2. Preheat the oven to 350°F. Line two baking sheets with parchment paper or silicone baking mats.

3. In a food processor fitted with a blade, grind 1 cup of the toasted pecans until coarsely chopped. Transfer to a small bowl and set aside. Add the remaining pecans to a food processor with the granulated sugar, salt, and cinnamon. Grind until the pecans are the texture of cornmeal. Add the vanilla. Chop the butter into 1-inch chunks and add to the food processor bowl. Process until the mixture forms into a smooth paste. Add the flour and pulse until the dough comes together.

4. Transfer the dough to a medium bowl. Mix in the reserved chopped pecans. Cover and refrigerate for 30 minutes.

Continued

5. Use a cookie scoop or tablespoon to portion the dough into 1½-inch balls. Line the cookies 1 inch apart on the prepared baking sheets.

6. Bake the cookies for 18 to 20 minutes, or until they just begin to brown around the edges. Let cool on the baking sheets for 5 minutes. Transfer to a wire rack and let cool for another few minutes until slightly warm but not too soft to pick up.

7. In a small bowl, add the confectioners' sugar. Roll the barely warm cookies in the sugar. Let cool completely, then roll in the sugar again.

VARIATION TIP: Add a teaspoon of grated lime zest and a pinch of cayenne pepper for a zesty flavor. For walnut cookies, use 2 cups of toasted walnuts in place of the pecans.

NEW YORK BLACK & WHITE COOKIES

Makes 12 cookies

If you have lived near or even visited New York City, you probably know what a black and white cookie is. It is more like a flat cake than a cookie, and it's iced with both vanilla and chocolate icing. That is great news, because it means you don't have to choose between the two flavors—you get both in one delicious treat. NUT-FREE

PREP TIME: 20 minutes
BAKE TIME: 15 to 20 minutes
EQUIPMENT: Baking sheets, parchment paper or silicone baking mats, whisk, mixing bowls, electric mixer, cookie scoop (optional)

FOR THE COOKIES

1½ cups (7.5 ounces, 210g) all-purpose flour
½ teaspoon salt
½ teaspoon baking powder
¼ teaspoon baking soda
¾ cup (6 ounces, 168g) granulated sugar
6 tablespoons (3 ounces, 85g) unsalted butter, at room temperature
¼ cup (1.5 ounces, 45g) vegetable shortening
1 large egg
3 tablespoons buttermilk
2 teaspoons vanilla extract

FOR THE ICING

2½ cups (10 ounces, 280g) confectioners' sugar
2 teaspoons light corn syrup
⅓ cup (3 ounces, 90 ml) hot water, divided
½ teaspoon vanilla extract
¼ cup cocoa powder

TO MAKE THE COOKIES

1. Preheat the oven to 350°F. Line two baking sheets with parchment paper or silicone baking mats.

2. In a small bowl, whisk together the flour, salt, baking powder, and baking soda.

3. In a large bowl, using an electric mixer, cream the sugar with the butter and shortening until light and fluffy. Add the egg, buttermilk, and vanilla, and mix until combined. Add the dry ingredients and mix just until combined.

Continued

4. Scoop or pipe the dough into 12 equal mounds. Arrange 6 cookies on each prepared baking sheet. Flatten the tops slightly so the cookies are the shape of small biscuits.

5. Bake for 15 to 20 minutes, or until the cookies are golden brown around the edges and set in the middle.

6. Transfer the cookies to a wire rack and let cool to room temperature.

TO MAKE THE ICING

1. In a small bowl, whisk together the confectioners' sugar, corn syrup, 4 tablespoons of hot water, and the vanilla until smooth and glossy. The icing should be the texture of thick pancake batter, spreadable but thin enough to smooth out as it settles.

2. In another small bowl, add the cocoa. Add half of the icing from the first bowl and a tablespoon of hot water. Whisk until smooth. If the icing is very thick, add a few more drops of water. If the icing becomes too runny, whisk in a little more confectioners' sugar.

3. Flip the cookies over so the flat side is up. Ice half of each cookie with vanilla icing and the other half with chocolate icing. Allow the icing to set before serving the cookies.

SUBSTITUTION TIP: If you don't have buttermilk available, you can use 3 tablespoons of whole milk mixed with ½ teaspoon of freshly squeezed lemon juice or white vinegar. Let the mixture sit for a minute to thicken.

PEANUT BUTTER & JELLY SANDWICH COOKIES

Makes 24 sandwich cookies

Kids of all ages love a good PB&J sandwich. This recipe turns our favorite sandwich into a cookie. Chewy cookies with a crunchy honey-roasted peanut topping, creamy peanut butter filling, and the jelly of your choice come together here for a deliciously tempting treat.

PREP TIME: 30 minutes

BAKE TIME: 10 minutes

EQUIPMENT: Baking sheets, parchment paper or silicone baking mats, whisk, mixing bowls, electric mixer, cookie scoop (optional), piping bag or spatula

FOR THE COOKIES

1 cup (8 ounces, 224g) honey-roasted peanuts, coarsely chopped

3 cups (14.5 ounces, 410g) all-purpose flour

1 teaspoon baking soda

1 teaspoon salt

2 sticks (8 ounces, 224g) unsalted butter, at room temperature

1 cup (8 ounces, 224g) granulated sugar

1 cup (8 ounces, 224g) lightly packed brown sugar

2 large eggs

2 teaspoons vanilla extract

1 cup (9 ounces, 255g) creamy peanut butter

FOR THE FILLING

1 stick (4 ounces, 115g) unsalted butter, at room temperature

½ cup (2.5 ounces, 70g) confectioners' sugar

⅔ cup (6 ounces, 168g) creamy peanut butter

2 teaspoons vanilla extract

½ cup grape or other flavor jelly

TO MAKE THE COOKIES

1. Preheat the oven to 375°F.

2. Put the chopped honey-roasted peanuts in a small bowl. Set aside.

3. Line three baking sheets with parchment paper or silicone baking mats. (Bake the cookies in batches if you only have one or two baking sheets.)

4. In a medium bowl, whisk together the flour, baking soda, and salt. Set aside.

Continued

5. In a large bowl, using an electric mixer, cream the butter with the granulated sugar and brown sugar until light and creamy. Mix in the eggs and vanilla. Mix in the peanut butter, scraping down the side of the bowl.

6. Add the dry ingredients and mix on low speed until the flour is partially incorporated. Increase the speed to medium and mix until all the flour is just combined.

7. Use a cookie scoop or tablespoon to portion the dough into 1½-inch balls. Press the top of each cookie ball into the chopped nuts, then place the cookie balls 2 inches apart on the prepared baking sheets.

8. Bake the cookies for about 10 minutes, or until the edges are beginning to brown and the tops are lightly puffed and still soft. Let cool for 10 minutes on the baking sheets before transferring to a wire rack. Let the cookies cool completely before filling them. They will collapse and crackle a little while cooling.

TO MAKE THE FILLING

1. In a large bowl, using the electric mixer, cream the butter with the confectioners' sugar until smooth. Mix in the peanut butter and vanilla, then use the mixer or whisk attachment to whip until light and fluffy.

2. Once the cookies have cooled completely, flip them over so they are flat-side up. Use a piping bag or small spatula to put a dollop of peanut butter filling on half of the flipped cookies. Spread jelly on the remaining cookies and sandwich them together.

VARIATION TIP: You can skip the filling and make plain peanut butter cookies. Or, for a special treat, try using hot pepper jelly in the filling.

BUTTERY SHORTBREAD COOKIES

Makes 24 cookies

Perhaps there is no better cookie than a simple shortbread cookie.
With only four ingredients and no vanilla or other flavoring, this cookie
is all about the butter. There's just enough flour to hold the dough
together, and just enough salt to emphasize the buttery flavor. Pour
a cup of tea and enjoy one of life's perfect little pleasures. NUT-FREE

PREP TIME: 20 minutes, plus 10 to
15 minutes chilling time

BAKE TIME: 10 to 15 minutes

EQUIPMENT: Baking sheets, parchment
paper or silicone baking mats, mixing
bowls, electric mixer, rolling pin

2 sticks (8 ounces, 224g) unsalted butter,
    at room temperature
½ cup (4 ounces, 112g) granulated sugar,
    plus more for sprinkling
¼ teaspoon salt
2 cups (10 ounces, 280g)
    all-purpose flour

MIXING TIP: When you cream the butter
and sugar, you don't want to incorporate
too much air. If the butter and sugar get
very aerated, the cookies will puff in the
oven. You want shortbread cookies to be
a little dense, with a melt-in-your-mouth
texture. Chilling the cookies briefly before
baking will prevent them from spreading
in the oven, so they'll maintain their shape
while baking.

1. Preheat the oven to 325°F. Line a baking
sheet with parchment paper or a silicone
baking mat.

2. Put the butter, sugar, and salt in a large
bowl. Using an electric mixer, mix for 2 to
3 minutes on medium speed until the
mixture is softened and blended, but not
very aerated.

3. Add the flour and mix just until a dough
forms. If the dough is very soft, chill briefly
to firm it up.

4. On a lightly floured surface, roll
the dough to a 10-by-10-inch square,
about ⅜ inch thick. Cut the dough into
24 rectangles.

5. Line the cookies ½ inch apart on the
prepared baking sheet. Using a fork, poke
three holes in each cookie. Sprinkle the
cookies with sugar, then refrigerate for
10 to 15 minutes.

6. Bake for 10 to 15 minutes, or until the
cookies are just set and barely beginning
to brown around the edges. Transfer to a
wire rack and let cool to room temperature.

RYE & CARAWAY WAFERS

Makes 48 cookies

This recipe is my adaptation of a traditional Swedish cookie. Traditionally, a small ½-inch hole is cut off-center in the cookie, and for the holidays, you can tie a ribbon through the hole in the cookie and use it as a tree decoration. If you don't like caraway seeds, you can sprinkle the cookies with coarse sugar instead. These cookies are not too sweet and have a special flavor from the rye flour. NUT-FREE

PREP TIME: 15 minutes

BAKE TIME: 12 to 14 minutes

EQUIPMENT: Baking sheets, parchment paper or silicone baking mats, whisk, mixing bowls, electric mixer, rolling pin, round cookie cutter (optional), pastry brush

1 cup (5.7 ounces, 160g) whole-grain rye flour

1½ cups (7.5 ounces, 210g) all-purpose flour

½ teaspoon salt

½ teaspoon ground cardamom

2 sticks (8 ounces, 224g) unsalted butter, at room temperature

½ cup (4 ounces, 112g) granulated sugar

1 egg white, beaten

Caraway seeds, for sprinkling

1. Preheat the oven to 375°F. Line two baking sheets with parchment paper or silicone baking mats.

2. In a small bowl, whisk together the rye flour, all-purpose flour, salt, and cardamom. Set aside.

3. In a large bowl, using an electric mixer, cream the butter and sugar until light and fluffy. Add the flour mixture and mix just until combined. If you're using a handheld mixer, the dough might look powdery, so use your hands to knead it together.

4. Turn the dough out onto a lightly floured surface and roll it out ⅛ inch thick. Use a 2½-inch round cookie cutter or the rim of a glass to cut out as many cookies as you can. Re-roll the scraps and continue cutting until all the dough is used.

5. Line the cookies ½ inch apart on the prepared baking sheets. Lightly brush each cookie with some of the egg white and sprinkle with caraway seeds.

6. Bake for 12 to 14 minutes, or until the cookies are just beginning to brown around the edges and are set in the middle.

7. Transfer the cookies to a wire rack and let cool to room temperature. The cookies will keep in an airtight container for about a week.

ROLLING TIP: Because of the rye flour, this dough is a little crumbly and may crack while you roll it. Use your hands to pinch the dough back together and keep rolling.

PALMIERS

≥ Makes 48 cookies ≤

Palmiers are also called elephant ears and pig's ears. The recipe is short on ingredients and a little longer on the listed steps. There aren't really that many steps to making these cookies; it just takes a bit of description to convey the technique for forming the crunchy, caramelized little treats. You can use the recipe for Quick Puff Pastry (page 144) or use store-bought frozen puff pastry sheets. NUT-FREE

PREP TIME: 15 minutes, plus 30 minutes chilling time
BAKE TIME: 10 to 12 minutes
EQUIPMENT: Rolling pin, baking sheets, parchment paper or silicone baking mats

½ recipe Quick Puff Pastry (page 144) or 2 sheets store-bought thawed frozen puff pastry
About ½ cup (4 ounces, 112g) granulated sugar

1. Liberally sprinkle a work surface with sugar. If using Quick Puff Pastry, divide the dough in half and work with one piece at a time. If using store-bought pastry, lay one sheet on the work surface. Roll the pastry into a 11-by-13-inch rectangle, about ⅛ inch thick. As you roll, sprinkle the sugar over the dough so it gets rolled into it.

2. Starting at one of the long ends, fold down the top 2 inches of pastry toward the middle. Repeat the fold on the other side of the dough so you now have both long ends folded toward the middle of the dough. Continue folding each end over itself until the two folds meet in the middle with a small gap in between. Close the two sides like a book. You should now have a log of dough that is made up of two rolls attached in the middle. Repeat this process with the other piece of dough (or the other sheet of store-bought pastry). Wrap the logs in plastic wrap and refrigerate for at least 30 minutes to firm up the dough.

3. Preheat the oven to 400°F. Line a baking sheet with parchment paper or a silicone baking mat.

4. Use a serrated knife to cut the logs into ½-inch-thick slices. Lay the cookies flat on the prepared baking sheet, 2 inches apart, so they have room to "puff."

5. Bake on the middle rack of the oven for 10 to 12 minutes, or until the cookies are golden brown on top and the bottoms are nicely caramelized.

6. Let the cookies cool on the baking sheet before transferring to a serving tray.

MAKE-AHEAD TIP: You can roll the dough and freeze the logs for up to a month before using. Let them thaw about half-way, then slice the cookies and bake.

CHECKERBOARD COOKIES

≥ *Makes 48 cookies* ≤

These adorable little cookies are not very difficult to make, but it does take several steps to create the checkerboard pattern that's designed to impress. This recipe makes a large batch of cookies, and the dough can be made ahead and frozen. Let thaw, then slice and bake when you're ready to enjoy. If at any point during preparation, the dough becomes too soft, allow it to chill in the refrigerator before proceeding. NUT-FREE

PREP TIME: 1 hour, plus 1 hour chilling time
BAKE TIME: 12 to 15 minutes
EQUIPMENT: Mixing bowl, electric mixer, rolling pin, pastry brush, baking sheets, parchment paper or silicone baking mats

3 sticks (12 ounces, 336g) unsalted butter, at room temperature
⅔ cup (6 ounces, 170g) granulated sugar
1 teaspoon salt
2 teaspoons vanilla extract
2½ cups (12.5 ounces, 350g) all-purpose flour
2 tablespoons Dutch process cocoa powder

1. In a large bowl, using an electric mixer, cream the butter with the sugar until creamy and well blended, but not fluffy. Add the salt and vanilla, then add the flour. Mix until just combined. Turn the dough out onto a lightly floured work surface and knead until a smooth ball forms.

2. Split the dough in half. Knead the cocoa powder into one half to make the chocolate dough. Wrap both pieces of dough in plastic and refrigerate for at least 30 minutes, or until firm.

3. Roll each piece of dough to a 6-by-12-inch rectangle, about ½ inch thick. Brush the surface of the chocolate dough with water, place the vanilla dough on top of the chocolate dough, and line up the edges. Trim each of the long sides of the dough to make straight edges, saving the scraps. Cut the rectangle lengthwise into three equal 2-inch slices. Brush the tops of two of the slices with water, then place

all three slices in a stack; the water will help them adhere. You should now have a 2-by-12-inch rectangle with six alternating layers of chocolate and vanilla. Once again, trim the long sides so they are straight, saving the scraps.

4. Slice the dough lengthwise into four ½-inch-wide slices. Lay one slice on its side with a vanilla stripe on the left side. Brush the slice with water. Lay the next slice on top of the first, flipping the slice so a chocolate stripe is on the left side, lined up with the vanilla stripe on the first slice. Brush the second slice with water and lay the next slice on top, vanilla stripe to the left. Brush with water and lay the final slice on so the chocolate stripe is to the left. The dough will resemble a square log.

5. Knead together the reserved dough scraps and shape into an 8-by-12-inch rectangle. Brush the rectangle with water and place the square log along one edge of it. Roll up so that the log is wrapped in the dough.

6. Wrap the log in plastic and chill until firm, at least 30 minutes. Alternatively, you can freeze the log for up to a month.

7. Preheat the oven to 350°F. Line a baking sheet with parchment paper or a silicone baking mat.

8. To bake, trim the uneven ends off the log. Use a sharp knife to cut to ¼-inch-thick slices. Line the cookies ½ inch apart on the prepared baking sheet. Bake for 12 to 15 minutes, or until the edges are beginning to brown and the cookies are set.

9. Transfer to a wire rack to let cool completely. The cookies will keep in an airtight container for up to a week.

SHORTCUT TIP: Instead of checkerboards, make these into swirl cookies. Roll the chocolate and vanilla dough each to a 12-by-12-inch square, ¼ inch thick. Lay the vanilla dough onto the chocolate dough, then slice the stacked square into three 4-inch-wide rectangles. Roll each rectangle up from the long side like a jelly roll. Chill, then slice and bake as directed.

APRICOT JEWEL COOKIES

Makes 32 cookies

I got this recipe from the very first pastry chef I worked for out of pastry school. The chef was Austrian, and he called these cookies "hussans." I have no idea what that means, but these have always been one of my favorite cookies. They are so simple and so good. NUT-FREE

PREP TIME: 15 minutes, plus at least 30 minutes chilling time

BAKE TIME: 12 to 15 minutes

EQUIPMENT: Mesh sieve, mixing bowl, electric mixer, baking sheets, parchment paper or silicone baking mats, pastry brush

¼ cup apricot preserves

½ cup (4 ounces, 112g) unsalted butter, at room temperature

½ cup (2 ounces, 56g) confectioners' sugar

2 egg yolks

½ teaspoon vanilla extract

¼ teaspoon lemon extract

1¼ cups (5.5 ounces, 155g) cake flour

1 egg, beaten, for egg wash

1. Put the apricot preserves in a microwave-safe bowl and heat in the microwave for about 30 seconds, then strain to remove the large pieces of fruit. Cover the preserves with plastic wrap and set aside to cool and solidify.

2. In a large bowl, using an electric mixer, cream the butter with the confectioners' sugar until light and fluffy. Mix in the egg yolks, vanilla, and lemon extract.

3. Add the flour and mix just until it is incorporated. Transfer the dough to a lightly floured work surface and knead into a ball. Form into an 8-inch log. Wrap the dough in plastic and refrigerate for at least 30 minutes or up to 2 days.

4. Preheat the oven to 350°F. Line a baking sheet with parchment paper or a silicone baking mat.

5. Remove the dough from the refrigerator and use your hands to roll it into a ¾-inch-thick dowel. If the dowel gets too long to handle, you can cut it in half and form two dowels.

6. Slice the dowel into 1½-inch-long segments. Line the cookies ½ inch apart on the prepared baking sheet. Use your thumb to make an indent in the middle of each cookie. Brush the cookies with the egg wash and spoon ¼ teaspoon of strained apricot preserves into each indentation.

7. Bake for 12 to 15 minutes, until the cookies are just beginning to brown around the edges.

8. Let the cookies cool on the baking sheet for 5 minutes, then transfer to a wire rack to cool completely.

VARIATION TIP: You can use any fruit preserves of your choice instead of the apricot.

PERFECTLY FUDGY BROWNIES

Makes 24 large or 32 small brownies

In the eternal battle of fudgy brownies versus cakey brownies, I vote 100 percent for fudgy. So, what makes a brownie fudgy as opposed to cakey? It's the amount of flour in the batter. With a mere cup of flour used in this recipe, these brownies are deliciously fudgy. NUT-FREE

PREP TIME: 10 minutes

BAKE TIME: 20 to 25 minutes

EQUIPMENT: 13-by-9-inch baking pan, parchment paper or aluminum foil, mixing bowl

9 ounces (255g) bittersweet
    chocolate, chopped
2 sticks (8 ounces, 224g) unsalted butter,
    cut into 1-inch chunks
1 cup (8 ounces, 224g) granulated sugar
½ cup (4 ounces, 112g) packed
    brown sugar
1 tablespoon vanilla extract
½ teaspoon salt
4 large eggs
1 cup (5 ounces, 140g) all-purpose flour

1. Preheat the oven to 350°F. Butter a 13-by-9-inch baking pan and line it with parchment paper or aluminum foil. If you use foil, butter the foil.

2. In a microwave-safe bowl, mix together the chopped chocolate and butter. Microwave for 1 minute, then stir to combine. Microwave in 30-second increments, stirring between increments, until all of the chocolate is melted. Add the granulated sugar, brown sugar, vanilla, and salt to the chocolate and stir to combine.

3. Add the eggs, stirring until incorporated, and then stir vigorously for another 30 seconds (see Tip). Add the flour and stir just until combined.

4. Pour the batter into the prepared pan and smooth into an even layer. Bake for 20 to 25 minutes, or until the brownies puff up a bit and a toothpick inserted in the center comes out with a few moist crumbs.

5. Let the brownies cool in the pan to room temperature, then refrigerate in the pan until they are firm.

6. Use the parchment paper or foil to lift the brownies out of the pan onto a cutting board. Cut into 24 large or 32 small squares. Lift each brownie off the parchment paper or foil and transfer to a serving platter.

TECHNIQUE TIP: Stirring the batter vigorously after adding the eggs will help form a crust on the top of the brownies. If you prefer a soft top, you can skip that step.

WHITE CHOCOLATE RASPBERRY BROWNIES

> *Makes 32 brownies*

Because they're made with white chocolate instead of dark chocolate, these brownies are not brown, but they are still brownies—if that makes sense. These truly delicious and surprisingly easy-to-make treats are studded with raspberries and white chocolate chips. The ivory color of the white chocolate is very striking against the bright-pink berries. And they are as tasty as they are pretty. NUT-FREE

PREP TIME: 20 minutes

BAKE TIME: 40 to 45 minutes

EQUIPMENT: 13-by-9-inch baking pan, parchment paper or aluminum foil, mixing bowl, whisk

2 cups (10 ounces, 280g) all-purpose flour

½ teaspoon salt

½ teaspoon baking powder

14 ounces (400g) white chocolate, chopped

2 sticks (8 ounces, 224g) unsalted butter

¾ cup plus 3 tablespoons (7 ounces, 196g) granulated sugar

4 large eggs

2 teaspoons vanilla extract

10 ounces (280g) white chocolate chips

1½ cups (7.5 ounces, 210g) frozen raspberries

1. Preheat the oven to 350°F. Butter a 13-by-9-inch baking pan and line it in both directions with parchment paper or aluminum foil. If you use foil, butter the foil.

2. In a small bowl, whisk together the flour, salt, and baking powder. Set aside.

3. Put the chopped white chocolate and butter into a large microwave-safe bowl. Microwave in 30-second increments, stirring between increments, until the white chocolate is melted.

4. Stir the sugar into the melted chocolate, then stir in the eggs and vanilla. Add the flour mixture and stir until it is completely incorporated. Fold in the white chocolate chips.

5. Pour the batter into the prepared pan and smooth into an even layer. Dot the frozen raspberries all over the surface of the batter, then gently push them into the batter.

6. Bake for 40 to 45 minutes, or until the brownies are golden brown and a toothpick inserted in the center comes out with a few moist crumbs but not raw batter.

7. Cool completely. Use the parchment paper or foil to lift and transfer the brownies to a cutting board. Remove the paper or foil, then cut into 32 squares.

INGREDIENT TIP: Make sure to use a high-quality white chocolate for the best flavor and texture.

BUTTERSCOTCH BLONDIES

Makes 32 blondies

The word "butterscotch" describes the flavor combination of brown sugar, butter, salt, and vanilla. By mixing these ingredients and binding them with just enough flour and eggs to hold everything together, we get a moist blondie with lots of butterscotch flavor. This recipe is so easy because it's made in one bowl and mixed by hand. NUT-FREE

PREP TIME: 20 minutes

BAKE TIME: 30 to 35 minutes

EQUIPMENT: 13-by-9-inch baking pan, parchment paper or aluminum foil, mixing bowl, spatula or wooden spoon

2 sticks (8 ounces, 224g) unsalted butter, melted

1 cup (8 ounces, 224g) granulated sugar

1⅓ cups (11 ounces, 308g) packed brown sugar

4 eggs

1 tablespoon plus 1 teaspoon vanilla extract

2 cups (10 ounces, 280g) all-purpose flour

¾ teaspoon salt

1. Preheat the oven to 350°F. Butter a 13-by-9-inch baking pan and line it in both directions with parchment paper or aluminum foil. If you use foil, butter the foil.

2. In a large bowl, using a wooden spoon or spatula, stir together the melted butter with the granulated sugar and brown sugar. Stir in the eggs and vanilla. Stir in the flour and salt.

3. Pour the batter into the prepared pan and smooth into an even layer. Bake for 30 to 35 minutes, or until the brownies puff up a bit and a toothpick inserted in the center comes out with a few moist crumbs but not raw batter.

4. Let the blondies cool completely in the pan. Use the parchment or foil to lift and transfer them to a cutting board. Remove the paper or foil, then cut into 32 squares.

CLEANUP TIP: Melt the butter in a microwave-safe bowl large enough to hold the batter. Then just add all the other ingredients to the same bowl after the butter is melted.

LEMON BARS

≥ Makes 24 bars ≥

What could be better than buttery shortbread topped with zesty lemon custard? Well, what's even better is how easy it is to make these bars. They're made in one bowl, and you don't even need a mixer. Ease and deliciousness: two good reasons these classic treats are so popular. NUT-FREE

PREP TIME: 30 minutes

BAKE TIME: 20 to 25 minutes

EQUIPMENT: 13-by-9-inch baking pan, parchment paper or aluminum foil, mixing bowl, spatula or wooden spoon, mesh sieve or sifter, rasp grater

FOR THE CRUST

2 cups (10 ounces, 280g)
    all-purpose flour
1 cup (8 ounces, 224g) granulated sugar
½ teaspoon salt
2 sticks (8 ounces, 224g) unsalted butter,
    at room temperature

FOR THE FILLING

1¼ cups (10 ounces, 283g)
    granulated sugar
3 tablespoons all-purpose flour
Pinch salt
4 large eggs
1 cup (8 ounces, 240 ml) freshly
    squeezed lemon juice (from 6 to
    8 lemons)
Finely grated zest of 2 lemons
Confectioners' sugar, for topping

TO MAKE THE CRUST

1. Preheat the oven to 375°F. Butter a 13-by-9-inch baking pan, then line it in both directions with parchment paper or aluminum foil. If you use foil, butter the foil.

2. In a bowl, combine the flour, sugar, and salt. Mix in the butter by hand, until it is incorporated and the pieces are no larger than pea-size. The dough will look powdery, but if you squeeze a handful, it will hold together as a large clump.

3. Dump the dough into the prepared pan and, using the palms of your hands, pat it into an even layer, making sure to get the corners. Bake until the crust is golden brown, about 15 minutes. Remove the pan from the oven and reduce the oven temperature to 325°F.

Continued

TO MAKE THE FILLING

1. In the same bowl you used for the dough, whisk together the granulated sugar, flour, and salt. Add the eggs and whisk until they are completely incorporated, with no pools of unmixed egg remaining. Add the lemon juice and zest, whisking to combine.

2. Pour the filling onto the warm crust in the baking pan and bake until the custard is set, 10 to 12 minutes. Give the pan a little shake. If the custard doesn't jiggle, it's ready. Let cool in the pan to room temperature, then refrigerate for at least 30 minutes.

3. Run a paring knife around the edges of the crust and use the parchment paper or foil to lift the dessert onto a cutting board. Peel back the edges of the paper or foil. Cut into 24 squares, wiping the blade of the knife with a damp cloth between cuts to get clean edges. Sift confectioners' sugar evenly over the bars, then lift each one off the parchment paper and transfer to a serving platter.

MIXING TIP: Make sure to mix the lemon filling in the order listed in the recipe. If you were to mix the eggs with the lemon juice without the protection of the other ingredients, they would be "cooked" by the acidic lemon juice.

CRANBERRY-ALMOND GRANOLA BARS

Makes 16 bars

Granola bars are a healthy and delicious treat that you can enjoy for breakfast or as a snack on the go. Homemade granola bars are fresher and tastier than premade, packaged bars. This recipe is chock-full of nuts, seeds, healthy oats, and protein-rich egg whites, so you can feel great about making these anytime the mood strikes. DAIRY-FREE

PREP TIME: 30 minutes

BAKE TIME: 20 to 25 minutes

EQUIPMENT: 13-by-9-inch baking pan, parchment paper (optional), food processor, mixing bowl, saucepan, whisk

1 cup (5 ounces, 140g) almonds

½ cup (2 ounces, 55g) wheat germ

¼ cup (1 ounce, 30g) sunflower seeds

¼ cup (1 ounce, 30g) pumpkin seeds

1 teaspoon ground cinnamon

½ teaspoon salt

2½ cups (8 ounces, 224g) old-fashioned rolled oats

1 cup (5 ounces, 140g) dried cranberries

½ cup (3.5 ounces, 105 ml) vegetable oil

½ cup (4 ounces, 112g) packed brown sugar

½ cup (4.5 ounces, 130g) almond butter

⅓ cup (4 ounces, 112g) pure maple syrup

2 large egg whites

1. Preheat the oven to 350°F. Brush a 13-by-9-inch baking pan with a thin coating of oil. Alternatively, line the pan with parchment paper to make the bars easier to lift out after baking.

2. In a food processor fitted with a blade, pulse the almonds a few times until coarsely chopped. Remove ½ cup of the almonds and set aside. Add the wheat germ, sunflower seeds, pumpkin seeds, cinnamon, and salt to the food processor. Pulse until the mixture resembles the texture of coarse cornmeal. Transfer to a large bowl and stir in the reserved chopped almonds, the oats and cranberries.

3. In a small saucepan, combine the oil, brown sugar, almond butter, and maple syrup. Cook over medium heat, stirring occasionally, until the almond butter and brown sugar are melted. Pour the brown sugar mixture over the oat mixture and stir to incorporate. Let cool to room temperature.

Continued

CRANBERRY-ALMOND GRANOLA BARS *Continued*

4. Whisk the egg whites by hand until quite frothy. Fold the whites into the granola. Pour the mixture into the prepared pan and press down into an even layer.

5. Bake for 20 to 25 minutes, or until golden brown around the edges and no longer sticky to the touch. Let cool in the pan for 10 minutes, then flip the pan to transfer the bars onto a cutting board. Alternatively, if you lined the pan with parchment paper, use it to lift the bars out of the pan and transfer to the cutting board. Cut into 16 bars and let cool completely. Store in an airtight container for up to a week.

VARIATION TIP: This is an endlessly adaptable recipe. Try swapping out the almonds for peanuts and the almond butter for peanut butter. You can also use raisins instead of cranberries, and honey in place of the maple syrup. Use any mix of seeds that you like.

RED VELVET CUPCAKES WITH
CREAM CHEESE FROSTING *pages 80 & 102*

CAKES, CUPCAKES & FROSTINGS

About Cakes

The three main types of cake recipes are butter cakes, sponge cakes, and chiffon cakes.

♦ **Butter cakes** are mixed with the creaming method. They have a buttery, melt-in-your-mouth texture.

♦ **Sponge cakes** rely on whipped eggs or egg whites for their structure. They are generally lower in fat content than a butter cake, and are often soaked with sugar syrup for flavor and moisture.

♦ **Chiffon cakes** are made with oil instead of butter. They're extra moist because they're made with a very wet batter.

Helpful Hints

♦ As mentioned, butter-based cakes are made using the creaming method. The traditional creaming method starts by beating together the butter and sugar. The sugar crystals' sharp edges cut through the butter to create lots of little air bubbles that will expand in the heat of the oven. The eggs are added one at a time, and the flour is added last. When the flour is added, it meets the liquid in the batter and causes gluten to form. With the traditional method, you need to take care not to mix the batter too much once the flour is added to avoid turning out a rubbery cake.

♦ Reverse creaming is an alternate technique used by many cake bakers, and it is the method used in this book. It's just as easy and fast as the traditional method, but it greatly reduces the chance of developing gluten and toughening the cake. Reverse creaming starts by beating together the flour, sugar, and butter. Mixing the butter with the flour coats the flour molecules with butterfat before the eggs and other liquids are added. This creates a barrier that slows the formation of gluten. Reverse creaming makes a cake with a very tender and velvety texture.

♦ Every butter cake recipe specifies that the butter and other ingredients should be at room temperature. Room temperature is 65° to 70°F. The butter must be at room temperature because it's difficult to whip air into cold butter during the creaming process. Room temperature batter will rise better in the oven and bake into a lighter cake.

Shortcuts/Time-Savers

◆ What if you forgot to take the butter and eggs out of the refrigerator ahead of time? There are a few shortcuts to bring them up to room temperature without having to wait all day:

◆ Eggs can be set in a bowl of warm tap water for a few minutes. They'll come up to room temperature very quickly.

◆ To help your butter warm faster, chop whole sticks of butter into 1-inch slices and set aside. After a few minutes, you can soften the butter with the paddle attachment on a stand mixer or with the beaters of a hand mixer before proceeding with the recipe. It's also possible to microwave the butter for very short increments. The butter should be flexible, but not completely softened and melting.

◆ Pan prep is much faster if you line the pan with parchment paper rather than greasing with butter and sprinkling with flour. This also saves on cleanup time. Even if you don't use parchment, save time by not greasing the sides of the pan. If only the bottom of the pan is greased, the cake will come out just fine and may even rise a little higher as it grips the ungreased sides of the pan.

VANILLA BUTTER CAKE

Serves 12

If you have just one cake recipe in your repertoire, this is the one to have. It makes a perfectly moist and buttery vanilla cake. Mixing the batter with the reverse creaming method (see page 74) ensures that your cake will always be soft and melt-in-your-mouth tender. This recipe can also be baked as 24 standard-size cupcakes. Cupcakes will take 12 to 14 minutes to bake. I like to fill and frost this cake with Italian Meringue Buttercream (page 105). NUT-FREE

PREP TIME: 30 minutes

BAKE TIME: 30 minutes, plus at least 3 hours chilling time

EQUIPMENT: Two 8-inch round cake pans, parchment paper (optional), mixing bowls, whisk, mesh sieve or sifter, electric mixer, spatula

6 large egg yolks, at room temperature
1 cup (8 ounces, 230g) sour cream, at room temperature, divided
1 tablespoon vanilla extract
1½ cups (12 ounces, 336g) granulated sugar, divided
2 cups (9 ounces, 252g) cake flour
¾ teaspoon salt
¾ teaspoon baking powder
¼ teaspoon baking soda
2 sticks plus 2 tablespoons (9 ounces, 255g) unsalted butter, at room temperature
3 large egg whites, at room temperature

1. Preheat the oven to 350°F. Line the bottom of two 8-inch round cake pans with parchment paper, or butter and flour the bottoms only of the pans.

2. In a small bowl, add the egg yolks, ½ cup of sour cream, and the vanilla. Whisk to combine.

3. Put 1¼ cups of sugar in a large bowl and sift in the flour, salt, baking powder, and baking soda. Using an electric mixer, mix on low speed to combine the ingredients. Add the butter and the remaining ½ cup of sour cream and mix on low speed until the butter is incorporated and the batter looks like a paste. Increase the speed to medium and mix for about 3 minutes, or until the batter lightens in texture. Use a spatula to scrape down the side and bottom of the bowl.

4. Add half of the egg yolk mixture and mix until mostly incorporated. Scrape down the side and bottom of the bowl, then add the rest of the egg yolk mixture. Mix until incorporated. Set aside.

5. In another large bowl, using the electric mixer, whip the egg whites on medium-high until soft peaks form. Slowly add the remaining ¼ cup of sugar and whip the whites to full peak. Fold the whites into the batter in two parts, folding in just until there are no visible streaks of egg white. Divide the batter between the two prepared pans and spread into an even layer.

6. Bake for 25 to 30 minutes, until the center of each cake springs back when lightly pressed or a toothpick inserted into the middle of each one comes out clean. Let cool for 10 minutes in the pans and then turn the cakes out onto a cooling rack.

7. When fully cooled, wrap each cake layer in plastic and refrigerate for at least 3 hours or overnight before filling and icing with your favorite frosting.

VARIATION TIP: To make Chocolate Butter Cake, use 1½ cups of cake flour and ½ cup cocoa powder instead of 2 cups of cake flour. Sift the cocoa with the other dry ingredients and mix as directed.

OLD-FASHIONED CHOCOLATE CAKE

⇒ Serves 12 ⇐

This cake is reminiscent of the quintessential chocolate layer cake that many of us grew up with. It's what you want to bake when you're craving the perfect slice of chocolate cake. It's a straightforward, easy-to-mix recipe, and it's the perfect partner for Old-Fashioned Chocolate Frosting (page 103). This recipe can also be baked as 24 standard-size cupcakes, which take about 20 minutes to bake. NUT-FREE

PREP TIME: 20 minutes

BAKE TIME: 30 minutes

EQUIPMENT: Two 8-inch round cake pans, parchment paper (optional), mixing bowls, whisk, mesh sieve or sifter, electric mixer (optional)

½ cup (2 ounces, 56g) Dutch process cocoa powder

½ teaspoon baking soda

½ cup (4 ounces, 120 ml) boiling water

2 cups (9 ounces, 255g) cake flour

1 teaspoon baking powder

½ teaspoon salt

2 cups (16 ounces, 455g) granulated sugar

1 cup (7 ounces, 210 ml) vegetable oil

4 large eggs

1 cup (8 ounces, 240 ml) buttermilk

1 tablespoon vanilla extract

1. Preheat the oven to 350°F. Line the bottom of two 8-inch round cake pans with parchment paper, or butter and flour the bottoms only of the pans.

2. In a small heatproof bowl, combine the cocoa and baking soda. Whisk in the boiling water, then set aside to cool.

3. Into a small bowl, sift the flour with the baking powder and salt. Set aside.

4. In a large bowl, add the sugar, oil, eggs, buttermilk, and vanilla. Mix with an electric mixer on medium speed or by hand with a wooden spoon to combine the ingredients. Continue mixing for 2 to 3 minutes to emulsify the ingredients.

5. With the mixer running on low, add the flour mixture, then add the cocoa mixture and mix until completely incorporated.

6. Divide the batter evenly between the two pans. Bake for about 30 minutes, until the top of each cake springs back when lightly pressed or a toothpick inserted in the middle of each one comes out clean.

7. Let the cakes cool in the pans for 20 minutes before turning out onto a wire rack. Let cool completely before filling and icing with your favorite frosting.

INGREDIENT TIP: Oil stays liquid at room temperature, so cakes made with oil are softer than ones made with butter.

RED VELVET CAKE

⇒ Serves 18 ⇐

Red velvet cake is thought to have originated in the southern United States. It's been around at least since the 1920s but has enjoyed renewed popularity over the last few years. This cake is especially wonderful filled and iced with either Cream Cheese Frosting (page 102) or the more traditional Ermine Frosting (page 104). NUT-FREE

PREP TIME: 30 minutes

BAKE TIME: 30 minutes

EQUIPMENT: Three 8-inch round cake pans, parchment paper (optional), mixing bowls, whisk, mesh sieve or sifter, electric mixer (optional)

3 cups (15 ounces, 430g) all-purpose flour

2 cups (16 ounces, 455g) granulated sugar

1½ teaspoons cocoa powder

1½ teaspoons baking soda

1 teaspoon salt

1¼ cups (9 ounces, 270 ml) vegetable oil

1 cup (8 ounces, 240 ml) buttermilk

3 eggs, at room temperature

1½ teaspoons vanilla extract

1½ teaspoons white vinegar

Red food coloring

BAKING TIP: If you don't have three cake pans, you can bake one-third of the batter in one pan and two-thirds in the other pan. When the cakes are completely cooled, split the larger cake horizontally into two layers. This recipe can also be baked as 24 standard-size cupcakes, which take about 20 minutes to bake.

1. Preheat the oven to 350°F. Line three 8-inch cake pans with parchment paper, or butter and flour the bottoms only of the pans.

2. In a bowl, sift together the flour, sugar, cocoa powder, baking soda, and salt. Set aside. In a large bowl, combine the oil, buttermilk, and eggs. Mix for a minute or two with an electric mixer or by hand with a wooden spoon to emulsify the ingredients. Add the vanilla, vinegar, and food coloring. If using gel coloring, use a few drops; if using liquid coloring, you may need the whole bottle. Tint to your preferred color.

3. Add the sifted dry ingredients to the wet ingredients and mix until completely blended.

4. Divide the batter evenly among the prepared pans. Bake for about 30 minutes, or until the middle of each cake springs back when lightly pressed.

5. Let the cakes cool in the pans for 10 minutes. Turn them out onto a wire rack and let cool completely before filling and icing with your favorite frosting.

CARROT CAKE

⩥ Serves 12 ⩤

I love the flavor of carrot cake, but I'm not a fan of its traditionally lumpy texture. Most carrot cake recipes use thickly shredded carrots, big raisins, and roughly chopped nuts. This one contains the typical ingredients, but the ingredients are prepared in a whole new way. It offers the great flavor and moisture of traditional carrot cake, but with a finer texture and beautiful deep-orange color. This recipe can also be baked as 24 standard-size cupcakes, which take 15 to 20 minutes to bake. DAIRY-FREE

PREP TIME: 30 minutes

BAKE TIME: 30 minutes

EQUIPMENT: Two to three 8-by-3-inch cake pans, parchment paper (optional), mixing bowls, food processor or grater, mesh sieve or sifter, electric mixer (optional)

1 cup (5 ounces, 142g) currants (optional)
1 pound (454g) carrots
2 cups (10 ounces, 280g)
   all-purpose flour
2 teaspoons baking powder
1 teaspoon baking soda
2 teaspoons ground cinnamon
2 teaspoons ground ginger
½ teaspoon ground nutmeg
½ teaspoon salt
1¼ cups (9 ounces, 270 ml) vegetable oil
1 cup (8 ounces, 224g) granulated sugar
1 cup (8 ounces, 224g) packed
   brown sugar
4 large eggs, at room temperature
1 tablespoon vanilla extract
1 teaspoon lemon extract
1 cup (8 ounces, 224g) walnuts, finely
   ground (optional)

1. Preheat the oven to 350°F. Line two or three 8-by-3-inch cake pans with parchment paper, or butter and flour the bottoms only of the pans.

2. If using the currants, place them in a bowl and pour 2 cups of hot water over them. Let soak for 20 minutes, drain, and set aside.

3. In a food processor, grind the carrots until the bits are very small but not quite a purée. Alternatively, shred the carrots on a grater, then use a knife to mince them into very small bits. Set the carrots aside.

4. In another bowl, sift together the flour, baking powder, baking soda, cinnamon, ginger, nutmeg, and salt. Set aside.

5. In a large bowl, using an electric mixer or hand whisk, mix the oil with the granulated sugar and brown sugar until the mixture resembles applesauce. Add the eggs, vanilla, and lemon extract. Mix until fully blended. Add the ground carrots and the currants and walnuts (if using).

Continued

6. Add the dry ingredients to the wet ingredients in three batches and mix until completely combined. Divide the batter evenly among the prepared pans.

7. Bake for about 30 minutes, or until each cake springs back when lightly pressed or a toothpick inserted in the center of each comes out clean. If you bake two layers instead of three, they may take a little longer to bake.

8. Let the cakes cool in the pan for 10 minutes, then turn them out onto a wire rack and let cool completely. Fill and ice with your favorite frosting.

INGREDIENT TIP: Indeed, the currants and walnuts are optional, but they add great flavor and moisture to the cake. This cake is decadent filled and iced with Cream Cheese Frosting (page 102). In fact, this is why I like to make three layers—so there's more filling—but two layers work well, too.

VELVETY WHITE CAKE

Serves 12

Have you ever taken a bite of a beautiful white layer cake only to be disappointed by a rubbery texture and bland taste? Given the proper ingredients and mixing technique, white cake can be soft and velvety with a perfect vanilla flavor. Thanks to the reverse creaming method (see page 74), it is possible to make a melt-in-your-mouth white cake—and here's the recipe. I like Italian Meringue Buttercream (page 105) with this cake. NUT-FREE

PREP TIME: 30 minutes
BAKE TIME: 25 to 30 minutes
EQUIPMENT: Two 8-inch round cake pans, parchment paper (optional), mixing bowls, mesh sieve or sifter, electric mixer, spatula

2 cups (10 ounces, 285g) cake flour
¾ teaspoon baking powder
¾ teaspoon salt
½ teaspoon baking soda
1½ cups (12 ounces, 340g) granulated sugar, divided
1 cup (8 ounces, 230g) sour cream, at room temperature, divided
2½ sticks (10 ounces, 283g) unsalted butter, at room temperature
1 tablespoon vanilla extract
6 egg whites, at room temperature

1. Preheat the oven to 350°F. Line two 8-inch cake pans with parchment paper, or butter and flour the bottoms only of the pans.

2. In a large bowl, sift the flour, baking powder, salt, and baking soda with 1 cup of sugar. Using an electric mixer, mix the dry ingredients on low speed for 30 seconds to distribute the leavening agents. With the mixer still on low speed, add ½ cup of sour cream, then add the butter a tablespoon at a time, mixing until combined. Add the remaining ½ cup of sour cream and the vanilla. Increase the speed to medium and beat for 3 to 4 minutes, or until the batter lightens in texture and becomes aerated. Use a spatula to scrape the side and bottom of the bowl to make sure there are no pockets of unmixed batter.

Continued

3. In another large bowl, with the electric mixer on medium-high speed, whip the egg whites until soft peaks form. Turn the mixer to medium-low speed and slowly add the remaining ½ cup of sugar. Turn the mixer to medium-high speed and whip the whites to full peak.

4. Fold the whites into the batter in three parts. Fold just until there are no streaks of egg white.

5. Divide the batter evenly between the prepared pans and spread to level. Bake for 25 to 30 minutes, or until the center

of each cake springs back when lightly pressed or a toothpick inserted into the middle of each comes out clean.

6. Let the cakes cool for 10 minutes in the pan, then turn out onto a wire rack. The cakes will settle a bit as they cool.

7. Once cool, trim the brown edges off the cakes and, if desired, split each one horizontally into two layers. Fill and ice with your favorite frosting.

BAKING TIP: This recipe can also be baked as 24 standard-size cupcakes, which take 12 to 14 minutes to bake.

STRAWBERRY TALL CAKE

Serves 12

A true strawberry shortcake is more like a biscuit than a cake (see page 36 for that recipe). What many folks call strawberry shortcake is actually a vanilla sponge cake layered with fresh strawberries and cream—that's what we're making here. This cake is amazingly delicious, completely gorgeous, and sentimental to me. This was my dad's favorite cake, and I made it every year for his birthday. NUT-FREE

PREP TIME: 30 minutes

BAKE TIME: 30 to 35 minutes, plus 1 hour to refrigerate

EQUIPMENT: Two 8-inch round cake pans, parchment paper (optional), mixing bowls, electric mixer, mesh sieve or sifter, piping bag (optional)

FOR THE CAKE

½ cup (3.5 ounces, 105 ml) vegetable oil

6 eggs, at room temperature, separated

¾ cup (6 ounces, 180 ml) water

1 tablespoon vanilla extract

2¼ cups (10 ounces, 285g) cake flour

1½ cups (12 ounces, 336g) granulated sugar, divided

1 tablespoon baking powder

½ teaspoon salt

FOR THE FILLING

1½ pounds ripe strawberries

¾ cup (6 ounces, 168g) granulated sugar, divided

1 to 2 tablespoons Grand Marnier liqueur or orange juice

2 cups (16 ounces, 480 ml) heavy cream

1 tablespoon vanilla extract

TO MAKE THE CAKE

1. Preheat the oven to 325°F. Line two 8-inch cake pans with parchment paper, or butter and flour the bottoms only of the pans.

2. In a large bowl, combine the oil, egg yolks, water, and vanilla. Using an electric mixer, mix on medium speed until well combined.

3. In a separate bowl, sift the flour with 1 cup of sugar, the baking powder, and salt. With the mixer on low speed, add the dry ingredients to the yolk mixture. Whip on high speed for 1 minute, then set aside.

4. In a separate bowl, whip the egg whites on medium-high speed until light and foamy. Gradually add in the remaining ½ cup of sugar and whip to full peaks. Fold the whites into the yolk mixture in three batches.

Continued

5. Divide the batter between the prepared pans and bake for 30 to 35 minutes, or until the middle of each cake springs back when lightly pressed.

6. Let the cakes cool in the pans for 10 minutes before turning out onto a wire rack. Let cool to room temperature before filling.

TO MAKE THE FILLING AND ASSEMBLE THE CAKE

1. Stem and reserve 6 good-looking strawberries of equal size. Stem and slice the remaining strawberries and place them in a large bowl. Mix with ½ cup of sugar and the Grand Marnier or orange juice. Set aside for at least 30 minutes.

2. In a large bowl, using the electric mixer, whip the cream with the remaining ¼ cup of sugar and the vanilla. Slice the top off of each cake to make them level. Cut each cake in half horizontally so you have four layers.

3. Place one layer on a serving platter and spoon one-third of the sliced strawberries and some juice on top. Spread the berries out to level. Spread one-quarter of the whipped cream over the berries, pushing the cream down in between them. Repeat to make two more layers, reserving some of the strawberry juice. Place the fourth cake layer on top of the last layer of filling and drizzle with the reserved strawberry juice. Frost the top of the cake with the remaining whipped cream. You can reserve ½ cup for decorating if you have a piping bag. Fit the bag with a star tip and pipe 12 rosettes around the top of the cake.

4. Slice the reserved strawberries in half and place one half, seed-side up, on each rosette. If you don't have a piping bag, just place the berries around the top of the cake decoratively. Wrap the sides of the cake so it doesn't dry out, and refrigerate for 1 hour before serving to allow the juices to absorb into the cake.

BAKING TIP: This is a chiffon cake recipe. Oil makes chiffon cake moist, and whipped egg whites make it light. This spongy cake will absorb lots of strawberry juice.

MEYER LEMON OLIVE OIL CAKE

Serves 16

Olive oil cake is a chiffon cake, meaning it's oil-based, with no butter in the batter. Because oil is liquid at room temperature, oil-based cakes are soft and moist, and have a very, very tender crumb. This cake gets even better after a day or two, which makes it the perfect make-ahead treat. DAIRY-FREE, NUT-FREE

PREP TIME: 20 minutes

BAKE TIME: 55 to 60 minutes

EQUIPMENT: 12-cup Bundt pan, mixing bowls, whisk, rasp grater, electric mixer

3 cups (14 ounces, 400g)
    all-purpose flour
½ cup (2.5 ounces, 70g) cornmeal
1½ teaspoons baking powder
½ teaspoon salt
2¼ cups (17 ounces, 485g)
    granulated sugar
1 pound (about 5) Meyer lemons
6 large eggs, at room temperature
1¼ cups (9 ounces, 270 ml) extra-virgin
    olive oil
Confectioners' sugar, for sprinkling

1. Preheat the oven to 350°F. Grease a 12-cup Bundt pan with baking spray or butter and flour the pan.

2. In a small bowl, combine the flour, cornmeal, baking powder, and salt, whisking together to distribute the baking powder. Set aside.

3. Put the granulated sugar in a large bowl. Finely grate the zest from all the lemons onto the sugar. Juice the lemons into another bowl to yield about ¾ cup of juice; set aside.

4. Using an electric mixer with the whisk attachment, mix the zest through the sugar on low speed. Add the eggs, increase the speed to medium-high, and whisk until the eggs thicken, become fluffy, and lighten in color. With the mixer still running, drizzle in the olive oil. Alternate adding the dry ingredients and the lemon juice to the batter, mixing well.

Continued

5. Pour the batter into the prepared pan. Bake for 55 to 60 minutes, or until the cake springs back lightly when pressed or a toothpick inserted in the center comes out clean. Let cool in the pan for 10 minutes, then invert onto a wire rack and let cool to room temperature. Sprinkle with a little confectioners' sugar before serving.

TECHNIQUE TIP: For this cake, you will "ribbon" the eggs with the sugar. This means that you whisk the eggs with the sugar until they aerate and lighten in color. By doing this, when you lift the whisk and drizzle the eggs back into the bowl, they'll leave a "ribbon" on the surface.

RUM CAKE

Serves 16

Some flavor compounds are alcohol-soluble, meaning that without alcohol, you won't taste them. So I often use a hint of liquor in my recipes. Usually alcohol is used sparingly to bring out other flavors, not to leave a "boozy" taste. This recipe is different. You are meant to taste the rum in this cake. The glaze is not shy with the liquor, so you get a sweet, rummy flavor in every bite. If you don't do alcohol, you can replace the rum with fruit juice. NUT-FREE

PREP TIME: 20 minutes

BAKE TIME: 35 to 40 minutes

EQUIPMENT: 12-cup Bundt pan, mixing bowls, whisk, mesh sieve or sifter, electric mixer, pastry brush

FOR THE CAKE

4 large eggs plus 2 yolks, at room temperature

¼ cup (2 ounces, 60 ml) vegetable oil

1 cup (8 ounces, 240 ml) buttermilk, divided

1 tablespoon vanilla extract

2½ cups (11.25 ounces, 315g) cake flour

1⅓ cups (10 ounces, 280g) granulated sugar

1 tablespoon baking powder

½ teaspoon salt

1½ sticks (6 ounces, 170g) unsalted butter, at room temperature, cut into 1-inch chunks

FOR THE RUM GLAZE

½ cup (4 ounces, 112g) unsalted butter

¼ cup (2 ounces, 60 ml) water

1 cup (8 ounces, 224g) granulated sugar

½ cup dark rum

TO MAKE THE CAKE

1. Preheat the oven to 350°F. Generously butter and flour a 12-cup Bundt pan or spray with baking spray.

2. In a small bowl, whisk together the whole eggs, egg yolks, oil, ½ cup of buttermilk, and the vanilla. Set aside.

3. Into a large bowl, sift the flour, sugar, baking powder, and salt. Using an electric mixer, mix on low speed to combine the dry ingredients.

4. Toss the chunks of butter into the flour mixture, then add the remaining ½ cup of buttermilk. Mix on medium-high speed for 2 to 3 minutes, or until fluffy. Use a spatula to scrape the side of the bowl and the beater. Add the egg mixture in three batches, scraping the bowl between each addition.

5. Pour the batter into the prepared pan. Bake for 35 to 40 minutes, or until the cake springs back when lightly pressed or a toothpick inserted in the center comes out clean.

Continued

TO MAKE THE RUM GLAZE AND ASSEMBLE THE CAKE

1. In a small saucepan, bring the butter, water, and sugar to a boil. Cook for 5 minutes, stirring constantly. Remove from the heat and stir in the rum.

2. As soon as the cake comes out of the oven, brush some of the glaze onto it. Let cool in the pan for 15 minutes to allow the glaze to absorb. Turn the cake out onto a wire rack set over a clean baking sheet.

3. Brush the entire cake with glaze, allowing it to absorb and repeating the brushing until all the glaze is used up. Let the cake cool completely before slicing.

MAKE-AHEAD TIP: This cake gets better after a day or two, so it's great to make in advance. Once the cake is completely cooled, wrap it tightly in plastic and let sit at room temperature until ready to serve. (It will keep at room temperature for 3 or 4 days.)

PERFECT VANILLA POUND CAKE

Serves 12

Pound cake is so named because the original recipe is made with 1 pound each of butter, sugar, flour, and eggs. Guess what? That recipe is not very good. It produces a cake that is dense and slightly rubbery. A great pound cake should have an even crumb with a melt-in-your-mouth texture and buttery vanilla flavor. This recipe will give you exactly that. NUT-FREE

PREP TIME: 20 minutes

BAKE TIME: 55 to 60 minutes

EQUIPMENT: 9-by-5-inch loaf pan or 12-cup Bundt pan, whisk, mixing bowls, mesh sieve or sifter, electric mixer

4 large eggs plus 3 yolks, at room temperature

1 teaspoon vanilla extract

¼ cup (2 ounces, 60 ml) whole milk, divided

1¾ cups (8 ounces, 224g) cake flour

1 teaspoon baking powder

¼ teaspoon salt

1¼ cups (10 ounces, 280g) granulated sugar

2 sticks plus 2 tablespoons (9 ounces, 255g) unsalted butter, at room temperature

TECHNIQUE TIP: This cake is made using the reverse creaming technique for an extra-tender texture. See page 74 for details about the benefits of this method and how it differs from the traditional creaming technique.

1. Preheat the oven to 350°F. Butter and flour a 9-by-5-inch loaf pan or a 12-cup Bundt pan.

2. In a small bowl, whisk together the whole eggs, egg yolks, vanilla, and 2 tablespoons of milk. Set aside.

3. Into a mixing bowl, sift the flour, baking powder, and salt. Add the sugar and whisk briefly to combine the ingredients.

4. Using an electric mixer on low speed, mix the butter into the flour mixture a tablespoon at a time. Add the remaining 2 tablespoons of milk. Increase the speed to medium-high and mix for 2 to 3 minutes. The batter will lighten in color and texture.

5. Scrape the bowl and beater thoroughly. With the mixer on low speed, add the egg mixture in three batches, scraping the bowl after each addition.

6. Pour the batter into the prepared pan and smooth until even. Bake for 55 to 60 minutes, until a toothpick inserted in the center comes out clean.

7. Let the cake cool in the pan for 10 minutes before turning out onto a wire rack. Let cool to room temperature before slicing.

ORANGE-CARDAMOM POUND CAKE

⸻ Serves 12 ⸻

This recipe is a variation of Perfect Vanilla Pound Cake (page 91). Adding sour cream to the batter makes the cake extra tender and ever so slightly tangy. Orange zest, orange extract, and cardamom give this pound cake an addictive, exotic flavor. NUT-FREE

PREP TIME: 20 minutes

BAKE TIME: 55 to 60 minutes

EQUIPMENT: 9-by-5-inch loaf pan or 12-cup Bundt pan, whisk, mixing bowls, mesh sieve or sifter, electric mixer, rasp grater

4 large eggs plus 3 yolks, at room temperature

1 teaspoon vanilla extract

1 teaspoon natural orange extract

½ cup (4 ounces, 112g) sour cream, divided

1¾ cups (8 ounces, 224g) cake flour

1 teaspoon baking powder

¼ teaspoon salt

1¼ cups (10 ounces, 285g) granulated sugar

Finely grated zest of 1 orange

1 teaspoon ground cardamom

2 sticks (8 ounces, 224g) unsalted butter, at room temperature

1. Preheat the oven to 350°F. Butter and flour a 9-by-5-inch loaf pan or a 12-cup Bundt pan.

2. In a small bowl, whisk together the whole eggs, egg yolks, vanilla, orange extract, and ¼ cup of sour cream. Set aside.

3. In a large bowl, sift together the flour, baking powder, and salt. Add the sugar, orange zest, and cardamom and, using an electric mixer, mix on low speed for 30 seconds.

4. With the mixer still on low speed, add the butter to the flour mixture a tablespoon at a time and mix until combined. Add the remaining ¼ cup of sour cream and increase the speed to medium-high. Mix for 2 to 3 minutes. The batter will lighten in color and texture.

5. Scrape the bowl and beater thoroughly. On low speed, add the egg mixture in three batches, scraping the bowl after each addition.

6. Pour the batter into the prepared pan. Bake for 55 to 60 minutes, until a toothpick inserted in the center comes out clean.

7. Let the cake cool in the pan for 10 minutes before turning out onto a wire rack. Let cool to room temperature before slicing.

INGREDIENT TIP: The zest of an orange has oils that contain more potent orange flavor than orange juice. Adding the zest directly to the sugar allows the sugar to absorb this orange oil for maximum flavor.

PEACH-ALMOND UPSIDE-DOWN CAKE

Serves 8

The middle of a peach pit has a bitter almond flavor, so peaches have a natural affinity with almonds. This batter contains almond meal for tenderness and almond extract for flavor. The cake is delicious still slightly warm from the oven, but the flavor of the cake is even better the second day.

PREP TIME: 30 minutes

BAKE TIME: 35 to 40 minutes

EQUIPMENT: Cast iron skillet or 9-inch cake pan (see Tip), mixing bowl, whisk, mesh sieve or sifter, electric mixer

FOR THE TOPPING

4 large peaches, pitted, peeled, and cut into 8 slices each

½ cup (4 ounces, 112g) packed brown sugar

½ teaspoon real almond extract

4 tablespoons (2 ounces, 60g) unsalted butter

FOR THE CAKE

1 egg plus 2 yolks, at room temperature

½ teaspoon real almond extract

½ cup (4 ounces, 120 ml) buttermilk, divided

1½ cups (6.75 ounces, 190g) cake flour

1½ teaspoons baking powder

¼ teaspoon salt

1 cup (8 ounces, 224g) granulated sugar

½ cup (2 ounces, 55g) almond meal or almond flour

1 stick (4 ounces, 112g) butter, at room temperature, cut into 1-inch pieces

TO MAKE THE TOPPING

Toss the sliced peaches with the brown sugar and almond extract. Allow to macerate for 30 minutes to an hour. Drain the peaches, reserving the juice. In a 9- or 10-inch cast iron skillet over medium heat (see Tip), melt the butter. Add the peach juice and bring the mixture to a boil. Let boil for 1 minute to thicken. Turn off the heat. Arrange the peach slices over the caramelized juice. Let the skillet cool completely while preparing the cake.

TO MAKE THE CAKE

1. Preheat the oven to 350°F.

2. In a small bowl, whisk together the whole egg, egg yolks, almond extract, and ¼ cup of buttermilk. Set aside.

3. Into a mixing bowl, sift the flour, baking powder, and salt. Add the sugar and almond meal. Using an electric mixer, mix on low speed for 30 seconds to combine the dry ingredients. Add the butter and mix until combined. Add the remaining ¼ cup of buttermilk. Mix on medium-high speed for 2 to 3 minutes to blend and aerate the batter. Add the egg mixture in two batches, scraping between additions.

4. Gently dollop the batter over the peaches in the cast iron skillet, and spread to cover all the fruit. Bake for 35 to 40 minutes, or until the center of the cake springs back when lightly pressed or a toothpick inserted in the center comes out clean.

5. Let the cake cool in the skillet for 10 minutes. To unmold, run a paring knife around the side of the cake to unstick it. Place a large serving plate over the pan and flip the cake onto the serving plate. If any caramel or peaches stick in the skillet, scrape them out with a small spatula and replace on the cake. Serve warm or at room temperature.

EQUIPMENT TIP: If you don't have a cast iron skillet, you can bake the cake in a 9-inch-square or round cake pan. If using a cake pan, butter and flour the bottom of the pan or line the bottom with parchment paper. Cook the butter and peach juices in a small saucepan, then pour into the prepared cake pan. Proceed as directed.

LEMON PUDDING CAKE

Serves 6

This pudding cake is kind of amazing. What looks like an ordinary crepe or pancake batter magically bakes into two separate and distinct layers of lemony goodness, and you don't have to do anything special to make it happen. For individual cakes, bake the batter in six 6-ounce ramekins. NUT-FREE

PREP TIME: 30 minutes

BAKE TIME: 30 to 35 minutes

EQUIPMENT: 9-inch square cake pan, mixing bowls, electric mixer, whisk, 13-by-9-inch baking pan, rasp grater

4 tablespoons (2 ounces, 55g) unsalted butter, at room temperature

1 cup (8 ounces, 224g) granulated sugar

¼ teaspoon salt

3 eggs, at room temperature, separated

1 tablespoon finely grated lemon zest

¼ cup (1.5 ounce, 40g) all-purpose flour

½ cup (4 ounces, 120 ml) freshly squeezed lemon juice (from 3 or 4 lemons)

1 cup (8 ounces, 240 ml) whole milk

½ teaspoon lemon extract

BAKING SCIENCE TIP: How does the magic happen? Because this batter is so wet, the air bubbles from the whipped egg whites cannot be held in place. As the cake bakes, those bubbles float to the top of the cake and bake into a spongy cake layer. Meanwhile, the egg yolks, butter, milk, and starch sink to the bottom and cook into a rich, custardy layer.

1. Preheat the oven to 325°F. Lightly butter a 9-inch-square pan and coat the inside with sugar.

2. In a bowl, mix the butter with the sugar and salt. Add the egg yolks and lemon zest, and mix until the batter comes together. Add the flour and mix until smooth. Slowly mix in the lemon juice, then add the milk and lemon extract. The batter will be very loose, with the texture of heavy cream.

3. Whip the egg whites to full peaks. Whisk one-third of the whites into the batter, then fold in the remaining whites in two batches.

4. Immediately pour the batter into the prepared pan. Set the pan into a larger 13-by-9-inch baking pan. Place on the oven rack and pour cold water into the larger pan until it comes halfway up the sides of the square pan.

5. Bake for 30 to 35 minutes, or until the center of the cake is set and springs back when lightly touched, but leaves a slight indentation in the cake. Remove the cake pan from the water bath and let cool on a wire rack. The cake can be eaten slightly warm, at room temperature, or chilled.

FLOURLESS CHOCOLATE CAKE

≥ Serves 8 ≤

This chocolate cake falls somewhere between a brownie and a cake. Because there is no flour in the batter, the cake is fudgy like a brownie. But the ground almonds act like flour and give the cake a little more structure than a brownie has. The eggs are whipped until they are light and airy, making this cake less dense than a brownie. GLUTEN-FREE

PREP TIME: 30 minutes

BAKE TIME: 25 to 30 minutes

EQUIPMENT: 9-inch cake pan, mixing bowls, electric mixer, whisk

1½ cups (5 ounces, 145g) almond flour or ground almonds (see Tip), divided

6 ounces (170g) semisweet chocolate, chopped

1 stick (4 ounces, 112g) unsalted butter, cut into 8 pieces

¾ cup (6 ounces, 168g) granulated sugar, divided

2 tablespoons dark rum

1 teaspoon vanilla extract

6 large eggs

¼ teaspoon salt

Whipped cream or vanilla ice cream, for serving (optional)

1. Preheat the oven to 350°F. Butter a 9-inch springform pan or regular cake pan and use 2 tablespoons of almond flour to dust it.

2. In a microwave-safe bowl, combine the chocolate and butter. Microwave for 1 minute, then stir. Continue microwaving and stirring in 30-second increments until the chocolate is melted.

3. Combine 1¼ cups of almond flour with ¼ cup of sugar. Stir this mixture into the chocolate mixture. Add the rum and vanilla.

4. Using an electric mixer on medium-high speed, mix the eggs, salt, and remaining ½ cup of sugar until the batter is tripled in volume and the color turns pale yellow. Using a whisk, fold one-third of the egg mixture into the chocolate mixture, then fold the chocolate mixture into the remaining egg mixture. Mix until no streaks of egg are visible.

5. Pour the batter into the prepared pan and sprinkle the remaining 2 tablespoons of almond flour evenly across the top.

Continued

6. Bake for 25 to 30 minutes, or until the cake is set and a toothpick inserted in the center comes out with a few wet crumbs.

7. Let the cake cool in the pan for 10 minutes. Run a knife around the side of the cake to unstick it, then release the springform pan. If you are using a regular cake pan, flip the cake onto a plate, then flip it again so it's right-side up.

8. Serve warm with a dollop of lightly sweetened whipped cream or a scoop of vanilla ice cream, if desired.

INGREDIENT TIP: Almond flour is made from ground almonds and can be used for any recipe that calls for ground almonds. You can grind your own almonds or use store-bought almond flour.

VANILLA CHEESECAKE

Serves 12

Cheesecake is actually more of a custard than a cake. But, since it's baked in a cake pan, we'll go ahead and call it a cake anyway. This cheesecake is rich and has a lovely, slightly tangy flavor because of the sour cream in the batter. I use a full tablespoon of vanilla in the batter to get a distinctively vanilla flavor. NUT-FREE

PREP TIME: 30 minutes
BAKE TIME: 1 hour 15 minutes
EQUIPMENT: 9-inch round cake pan or springform pan, parchment paper or aluminum foil, mixing bowls, electric mixer, 13-by-9-inch baking pan

FOR THE CRUST

1½ cups (8 ounces, 225g) graham cracker crumbs (about 14 crackers)
¼ cup (2 ounces, 56g) granulated sugar
6 tablespoons (3 ounces, 90g) butter, melted

FOR THE CHEESECAKE

3 (8-ounce) packages (24 ounces, 672g) cream cheese, at room temperature
1½ cups (12 ounces, 336g) granulated sugar
1 cup (8 ounces, 230g) sour cream, at room temperature
1 tablespoon vanilla extract
5 large eggs, at room temperature

TO MAKE THE CRUST

1. Preheat the oven to 350°F. Line the bottom of a 9-inch round cake pan or springform pan with parchment paper. If using a springform, wrap the outside with aluminum foil.

2. In a large bowl, combine the graham cracker crumbs and sugar. Sprinkle the melted butter over the crumbs and toss to combine. Press the crumbs into the bottom of the prepared pan. Bake for about 10 minutes, or until fragrant and lightly browned. Set aside to cool. Reduce the oven temperature to 325°F.

TO MAKE THE CHEESECAKE

1. Using an electric mixer on low speed, mix the cream cheese and sugar until well combined and no lumps remain. Scrape the bowl and beater. Add the sour cream and vanilla, and mix to combine.

Continued

2. With the mixer still on low speed, add the eggs in two batches, scraping the bowl and beater between additions (see Tip). Pour the batter into the crust in the cake pan. Set the pan into a larger pan and pour warm water into the larger pan until it comes halfway up the side of the cake pan.

3. Bake the cheesecake in the water bath for about 1 hour and 15 minutes, or until it is mostly set. The center of the cheesecake will still jiggle a bit. Set on a rack to cool to room temperature, then refrigerate for several hours or overnight, until completely firm.

4. If you used a springform pan, run a paring knife around the cheesecake to separate it from the pan, release the spring, and remove the pan. If you used a regular cake pan, dip the pan in a bowl of very hot water until the water is just below the lip of the pan. Lift the pan out of the water and run a knife or spatula around the side of the cheesecake, and flip it out onto a flat plate, then flip right-side up onto a serving platter. Keep refrigerated until ready to serve.

MIXING TIP: Once the eggs are added to the batter, take care not to mix too much. If you mix air into the eggs, the cheesecake will puff up in the oven and can crack.

AMERICAN BUTTERCREAM

Makes 3 cups

A recipe doesn't get any easier than this. American buttercream is the simplest frosting you can make. You can add a little more or a little less cream to get a thicker or thinner consistency. This buttercream is sweeter than either Italian Meringue Buttercream (page 105) or Ermine Frosting (page 104). This is definitely a kid-friendly recipe. GLUTEN-FREE, NUT-FREE

PREP TIME: 10 minutes

EQUIPMENT: Electric mixer, mixing bowl, spatula

2 sticks (8 ounces, 224g) unsalted butter, at room temperature

4 cups (16 ounces, 443g) confectioners' sugar

¼ teaspoon salt

3 tablespoons heavy cream

1 tablespoon vanilla extract

1. Using an electric mixer, cream the butter on medium speed until it is softened and becoming fluffy. With the mixer on low speed, slowly add the confectioners' sugar and mix until completely blended. Scrape the bowl.

2. Switch to the whisk attachment (if possible), add the salt, cream, and vanilla, and whip until light and airy.

3. Use the buttercream right away or store, covered, in the refrigerator until ready to use. Return to room temperature and re-whip before using.

VARIATION TIP: For lemon buttercream, add the zest of 1 lemon and a teaspoon of lemon extract. For coffee buttercream, add a tablespoon of instant espresso powder to the cream and warm in the microwave until the powder is melted. Let cool before adding to the buttercream.

CREAM CHEESE FROSTING

Makes 4 cups

Most cream cheese frosting recipes direct you to cream the butter, cream cheese, and sugar all together. However, the sugar is likely to absorb moisture from the cream cheese, making the frosting runny. This version starts by softening the butter, then adding the sugar, and finally the cream cheese. Not only does mixing this way prevent the sugar from absorbing too much moisture, it also allows the butter to become similar in texture to the cream cheese before the two are combined. So no lumps, ever! GLUTEN-FREE, NUT-FREE

PREP TIME: 20 minutes

EQUIPMENT: Electric mixer, mixing bowl, spatula

2 sticks (8 ounces, 224g) unsalted butter, at room temperature

2½ cups (10 ounces, 280g) confectioners' sugar

1 cup (8 ounces, 224g) cream cheese, at room temperature

1 tablespoon vanilla extract

1 teaspoon freshly squeezed lemon juice

1. In a large bowl, using an electric mixer, cream the butter until softened and slightly aerated. Slowly add the confectioners' sugar and mix until well blended, with no lumps of butter. Scrape the bowl and the beaters.

2. With the mixer on low speed, add the cream cheese a few tablespoons at a time. Add the vanilla and lemon juice.

3. Switch to the whisk attachment (if possible) and whip the mixture until light and fluffy.

STORAGE TIP: This frosting is best used immediately after it's made. A cake or cupcake frosted with cream cheese icing should be refrigerated until serving.

OLD-FASHIONED CHOCOLATE FROSTING

Makes enough to fill and frost an 8-inch cake

This is a simple and delicious chocolate frosting. Cocoa gives this buttercream a lovely fudgy flavor. It's the perfect frosting for Old-Fashioned Chocolate Cake (page 78). GLUTEN-FREE, NUT-FREE

PREP TIME: 20 minutes
EQUIPMENT: Microwave-safe bowls, electric mixer, mixing bowl

½ cup (2 ounces, 56g) Dutch process cocoa powder
½ cup (4 ounces, 120 ml) whole milk
1 tablespoon vanilla extract
⅛ teaspoon salt
2 sticks (8 ounces, 224g) unsalted butter, at room temperature
3½ cups (14 ounces, 392g) confectioners' sugar

1. Place the cocoa in a small heatproof bowl. In a separate microwave-safe container, combine the milk, vanilla, and salt. Microwave in 10-second increments until the milk is almost boiling. Pour the warm milk over the cocoa and whisk until smooth. Set aside to cool completely.

2. In a large bowl, using an electric mixer, cream the butter on medium speed until it is softened and beginning to aerate. With the mixer on low speed, slowly add the confectioners' sugar, mixing until completely combined. Add the cooled cocoa mix, switch to the whisk attachment (if possible), and whip until the frosting is light and fluffy.

3. Use the frosting immediately, or store in the refrigerator until ready to use and re-whip before using.

INGREDIENT TIP: Mixing the cocoa with the hot milk will "bloom" the cocoa, releasing more of the pure chocolate flavor. This simple step gives the buttercream a deeper chocolate richness.

ERMINE FROSTING

Makes enough to fill and frost an 8-inch cake

I love this old-fashioned buttercream recipe, which is less sweet than American Buttercream (page 101), but a little sweeter than Italian Meringue Buttercream (page 105). Because the sugar is cooked into the pudding-like base, there is no grittiness in this frosting. It's a traditional filling and frosting for Red Velvet Cake (page 80). NUT-FREE

PREP TIME: 15 minutes

COOK TIME: 3 to 4 minutes

EQUIPMENT: Saucepan, whisk, electric mixer, mixing bowl

1½ cups (12 ounces, 336g) granulated sugar

½ cup (4 ounces, 112g) all-purpose flour

¼ teaspoon salt

1½ cups (12 ounces, 360 ml) whole milk

1 tablespoon vanilla extract

3 sticks (12 ounces, 336g) unsalted butter, at room temperature

1. In a small saucepan, whisk together the sugar, flour, and salt. Slowly whisk in the milk until smooth. Heat the mixture over medium-low heat, whisking constantly, until it begins to boil. Continue to cook and stir for 1 to 2 minutes, or until it thickens to a pudding-like texture. Immediately remove from the heat. Transfer to a small bowl, stir in the vanilla, and let cool to room temperature.

2. In a large bowl, using an electric mixture, cream the butter until light and fluffy. Add the milk mixture, a tablespoon at a time, until completely incorporated. Switch to the whisk attachment (if possible) and whip the buttercream until light and fluffy. Use immediately.

STORAGE TIP: Because there is milk in the frosting, it should be stored in the refrigerator. Remove frosted cake or cupcakes from the refrigerator 1 hour before serving so the frosting has time to soften.

ITALIAN MERINGUE BUTTERCREAM

Makes enough to fill and frost an 8-inch cake

Light, fluffy, and not too sweet, this buttercream is a dream to work with. It has the perfect balance of rich flavor from the butter and lightness from the meringue. It's not overly sweet, and it can be flavored with an endless variety of creative add-ins. It's strong enough to pipe buttercream roses and stays soft at room temperature, so it melts in your mouth. You'll need a thermometer to check the syrup temperature (see Tip). Don't be intimidated—it's easy and the result is well worth it! GLUTEN-FREE, NUT-FREE

PREP TIME: 30 minutes
COOK TIME: 10 minutes
EQUIPMENT: Saucepan, whisk, electric mixer, mixing bowl, kitchen thermometer

¼ cup (60 ml) water
1 cup (8 ounces, 224g) granulated sugar, divided
5 large (6 ounces, 170g) egg whites, at room temperature
Pinch salt
4 sticks (16 ounces, 453g) unsalted butter, at room temperature, cut into 16 pieces
1 tablespoon vanilla extract

1. In a small saucepan, combine the water with ¾ cup of sugar. Cook on medium-high heat, stirring, until the sugar is melted. Once the syrup begins to boil, do not stir. Allow the syrup to cook to 235° to 240°F (soft ball stage).

2. While the syrup is boiling, using an electric mixer with the whisk attachment, whip the egg whites on medium-high speed. When the whites have soft peaks, reduce the mixer to medium-low and slowly add the remaining ¼ cup of sugar and the salt. Increase the speed to medium-high and whip to full peaks. Turn the mixer speed to medium and keep it running until the syrup is ready.

Continued

3. As soon as the syrup is at the correct temperature, remove the pan from the heat. With the mixer running on medium-low, pour the hot syrup in a steady stream between the edge of the bowl and the beater. Increase the speed to medium-high and continue whisking until the whites are cooled to about 80°F.

4. When the whites have cooled, with the mixer running on medium speed, add the butter, one piece at a time. Add the vanilla, increase the speed to medium-high, and whip until the buttercream comes together.

5. Store at room temperature until ready to use.

EQUIPMENT TIP: Traditionally, a special candy thermometer is used to check the temperature of sugar syrup. But there is no need to buy a special piece of equipment just for this. Any digital probe thermometer will work for this recipe. If you have a thermometer with a probe attached to a wire, just set the probe in the syrup and set the alarm for 235°F.

CHOCOLATE GANACHE

Makes 2 cups

Ganache has the pure flavor of a good semisweet chocolate, with a soft and creamy texture. Eating it is like eating chocolate silk. A staple in every pastry kitchen, ganache is used for glazing and filling cakes and cookies, making candies, as a tart filling, and as an ice cream sauce. The possibilities are endless. GLUTEN-FREE, NUT-FREE

PREP TIME: 15 minutes

BAKE TIME: 5 minutes

EQUIPMENT: Food processor (optional), microwave-safe bowl, mixing bowl, wooden spoon

8 ounces (225g) semisweet chocolate

1 tablespoon (.5 ounce, 15g)
   unsalted butter

1 cup (8 ounces, 240 ml) heavy cream

2 tablespoons light corn syrup (optional, for smoothness and glossiness)

1. Chop the chocolate into small pieces, no larger than ½ inch, or chop roughly and finish chopping in a food processor. Place the butter in a bowl (or in the food processor bowl) with the chocolate.

2. Pour the cream into a microwave-safe container and heat in the microwave until just below the boiling point, 2 to 3 minutes (see Tip).

3. Pour the cream all at once over the chocolate. Let sit without stirring for 1 to 2 minutes to allow the chocolate to begin melting.

4. Gently stir the chocolate with a wooden spoon, trying not to incorporate any air, until all the chocolate bits are melted. If using the food processor, run the processor for 20 to 30 seconds until the chocolate is melted. Stir in the corn syrup (if using).

5. Let the ganache cool to room temperature; it will set up as it cools.

Continued

HOW TO USE GANACHE:

1. *To make truffles*, let ganache firm up in the refrigerator. Scoop into 1-inch balls, then roll the balls in cocoa.

2. *To glaze a cake*, warm the ganache until it's a liquid, then pour it over a chilled cake set on a cooling rack.

3. *To make whipped ganache*, warm the ganache to room temperature so it's soft but not completely liquefied. Whip the ganache until it becomes lighter in color and aerated. Use whipped ganache to fill a cake or frost cupcakes.

4. *Pour ganache into a tart shell* and refrigerate until set. Top with whipped cream and serve for dessert.

INGREDIENT TIP: The time it takes for the cream to heat to just below boiling will depend on your microwave. Mine takes 2 to 3 minutes for a cup of cream.

BLUEBERRY COBBLER IN A
CAST IRON SKILLET *page 134*

PIES & TARTS

QUICK TUTORIAL

About Pies and Tarts

Both pies and tarts are, basically, crusts that encase a filling. So what's the difference? Mostly, it's the shape of the pan in which they're baked.

A pie is baked in a specific type of pan, usually 9 to 10 inches across and with sloping sides. Deep-dish pie pans have deeper sides than a standard pie pan.

A tart is generally baked in a shallow pan with straight sides. The sides of a basic tart pan are often fluted, and the bottom of the pan is removable.

Another type of tart, a galette, is free-form. The crust is formed by hand, without a pan.

Pies, tarts, and galettes can have either sweet or savory fillings, and the crusts can be formed with many different types of dough.

Helpful Hints

◆ Gather a few reliable dough recipes and use them for all your pies and tarts. Flaky pie dough can be used for sweet or savory recipes, and a good sweet crust can be used with many different sweet fillings.

◆ For a great piecrust, mixing the fat in two stages results in a dough that bakes up both flaky and tender.

◆ All tart and pie doughs should be chilled before rolling. To roll pie or tart dough evenly, roll from the center out and avoid rolling over the edges. Lift and move the dough frequently to ensure it's not sticking.

◆ I prefer a tapered French rolling pin because the tapered ends help you avoid rolling over the edges of the dough. I like the control of a rolling pin without handles.

Shortcuts/Time-Savers

◆ Mixing dough in a food processor is very quick and easy.

◆ Cutting cold butter into slices makes it easier to mix into flour for a flaky crust.

◆ If you're short on time, make a galette instead of a pie. Galettes are easier to make than pies because they are completely free-form.

◆ As long as you're mixing some dough, make an extra batch and put it in the freezer. Making a double batch doesn't take twice as long, so it will save time for your next dish.

FLAKY PIE DOUGH

Makes 1 1/2 pounds

Despite the old saying "easy as pie," many people are hesitant to make their own piecrust. Even people who do lots of baking often buy premade dough. Homemade piecrust is not difficult to make, it just takes a little finesse and patience. This recipe makes enough dough for a double-crust pie. NUT-FREE (CAN BE MADE VEGAN: SEE TIP)

PREP TIME: 20 minutes, plus 2 to 3 hours to chill

EQUIPMENT: Mixing bowls, whisk

2 cups (10 ounces, 285g) all-purpose flour

2/3 cup (3.5 ounces, 100g) cake flour

1 tablespoon granulated sugar

1 teaspoon salt

1/2 cup (4 ounces, 112g) vegetable shortening, cold

1 stick (4 ounces, 112g) unsalted butter, very cold and sliced into 1/4-inch-thick slices

1/2 cup (4 ounces, 120 ml) ice water

1/2 teaspoon apple cider vinegar

INGREDIENT TIP: Adding the fat in two stages ensures that your piecrust will be both tender and flaky. Adding the shortening first coats the flour to prevent gluten from developing. Keeping the butter in large pieces separates the layers of dough to create a flaky texture. To make a vegan piecrust, omit the butter and use 1 cup vegetable shortening. Add the shortening in two stages as described in the recipe.

1. In a large bowl, using a whisk, mix together the all-purpose flour, cake flour, sugar, and salt.

2. Using your fingers, cut the shortening into the flour mixture until it resembles coarse cornmeal. Next, quickly work in the butter so it doesn't get too soft. Don't break the butter down completely; leave some larger flakes remaining.

3. Mix the water with the cider vinegar. Make a well in the middle of the dry ingredients and pour the liquid in all at once. Toss until most of the liquid is absorbed. Gently press the dough until it comes together. It will look a little dry in spots. The water will redistribute in the dough as it rests.

4. Form the dough into a disk, wrap in plastic, and refrigerate for at least 2 to 3 hours before using. The dough can also be frozen for up to 3 months.

CREAM CHEESE PIE DOUGH

Makes 1 ½ pounds

This dough is terrific for hand pies. It's very easy to roll and sturdy enough to encase a filling. A little bit of sugar adds flavor and helps the crust brown. The cream cheese not only adds fat by replacing shortening, but it also imparts a wonderful slightly tangy flavor. This recipe makes enough dough for a double-crust pie. NUT-FREE

PREP TIME: 20 minutes, plus 2 to 3 hours to chill
EQUIPMENT: Mixing bowls, whisk

2 cups (10 ounces, 285g) all-purpose flour
⅔ cup (3.5 ounces, 100g) cake flour
1 tablespoon granulated sugar
½ teaspoon salt
½ cup (4 ounces, 112g) cream cheese, cut into 1-inch chunks
1 stick (4 ounces, 112g) cold unsalted butter, cut into 1-inch chunks
½ cup (4 ounces, 120 ml) ice water
½ teaspoon apple cider vinegar

INGREDIENT TIP: This recipe uses a mixture of all-purpose and cake flour to mimic pastry flour. All-purpose flour will give the dough enough structure so it can maintain a flaky texture, and cake flour helps keep it tender.

1. In a large bowl, whisk together the all-purpose flour, cake flour, sugar, and salt. Add the cream cheese and, using your fingers, mix it into the flour until it resembles coarse cornmeal. Add the butter and squeeze the chunks into "flakes," then break the flakes down into slightly smaller pieces, working quickly so the butter doesn't get soft. Don't break the butter down completely; leave some large flakes remaining.

2. In a small bowl, combine the water and cider vinegar. Make a well in the middle of the dry ingredients and pour the liquid into the flour all at once, mixing to combine. Gently work the dough just until it comes together. It may look a little dry in spots, but the water will redistribute as the dough rests.

3. Fold the dough into a disk, wrap in plastic, and refrigerate for at least 2 to 3 hours. The dough can also be frozen for up to 3 months.

SHORT DOUGH

Makes 1 pound

This is a basic dough recipe that's great to have in your collection, and it comes together in minutes. It's a little less sweet than a sugar cookie dough and a little less rich than shortbread dough—and, yes, it can be used for baking cookies, too. This is the dough I use to roll tart shells. It bakes up with a nice crisp bite and is strong enough to hold soft fillings like pastry cream or fresh fruit without getting soggy. This recipe makes enough dough for one 10- to 12-inch tart shell. NUT-FREE

PREP TIME: 10 minutes, plus 1 hour to chill
EQUIPMENT: Mixing bowls, electric mixer

1 stick plus 2 tablespoons (5 ounces, 140g) unsalted butter, at room temperature
⅓ cup (3 ounces, 84g) granulated sugar
1 egg yolk, at room temperature
½ teaspoon vanilla extract
1½ cups (7.5 ounces, 210g) all-purpose flour
¼ teaspoon salt

1. In a large bowl, using an electric mixer, cream the butter and sugar just until combined and slightly aerated (see Tip). Add the egg yolk and vanilla, mixing to combine, and scrape down the bowl and beaters.

2. Add the flour and salt, and mix until the dough barely comes together. Transfer the dough to a lightly floured work surface. Finish mixing by hand and knead the dough into a ball.

3. Flatten the ball into a disk, wrap in plastic, and refrigerate for at least 1 hour before using. The dough can also be frozen for up to 3 months.

MIXING TIP: You don't want to whip too much air into the butter and sugar for short dough. If the dough gets very aerated, the tart crust will be more crumbly than crisp, and crisp is what you want for a good crust that will hold softer fillings.

CHOCOLATE SHORT DOUGH

Makes 1 pound

This is a variation of regular Short Dough (page 115). There is a little more sugar used in this recipe to offset the slightly bitter edge of the cocoa. This is a wonderful dough for making chocolate tarts. It can also be rolled and cut as cookies. Dip half of the baked cookies in white or dark chocolate for a simple but decadent treat. This recipe makes enough dough for one 10- to 12-inch tart shell. NUT-FREE

PREP TIME: 10 minutes, plus 1 hour to chill

EQUIPMENT: Mixing bowls, whisk, electric mixer

1 cup (5 ounces, 140g) all-purpose flour

½ cup (2 ounces, 56g) Dutch process cocoa powder

¼ teaspoon salt

1 stick plus 2 tablespoons (5 ounces, 140g) unsalted butter, at room temperature

½ cup (4 ounces, 112g) granulated sugar

1 egg yolk, at room temperature

½ teaspoon vanilla extract

1. In a small bowl, whisk together the flour, cocoa, and salt. Set aside.

2. In a large bowl, using an electric mixer, cream the butter and sugar just until combined and slightly aerated. Add the egg yolk and vanilla, mixing to combine, and scrape down the bowl and beaters.

3. Add the dry ingredients and mix until the dough barely comes together. Transfer to a lightly floured work surface. Finish mixing by hand and knead the dough into a ball.

4. Flatten the ball into a disk, wrap in plastic, and refrigerate for at least 1 hour before using. The dough can also be frozen for up to 3 months.

INGREDIENT TIP: Because cocoa contains starch and protein, it will absorb water and contribute to the structure of a baked good. This is exactly what flour does, though flour adds even more structure than cocoa. For this reason, you can replace some of the flour in almost any recipe with an equal amount of cocoa to create a chocolate version of that recipe.

APPLE PIE

Serves 8

All-American apple pie needs no introduction, does it? I will say this: The perfect apple for apple pie is one that is both sweet and sour and has a firm texture that won't fall apart while baking. You may need to adjust the amount of sugar in the recipe based on which apples you use, so feel free to taste as you go. Granny Smith apples are widely available and are always a good option for baking. NUT-FREE

PREP TIME: 30 minutes active, 2 hours inactive

BAKE TIME: 1 hour

EQUIPMENT: 9-inch deep-dish pie plate, mixing bowls, rolling pin, whisk, saucepan, pastry brush, baking sheet

3 pounds (1.3 kg) apples, cored, peeled, and sliced ¼ inch thick

½ to ¾ cup (4 to 6 ounces, 112g to 168g) granulated sugar, plus more for sprinkling

Pinch salt

1 recipe Flaky Pie Dough (page 113)

2 tablespoons (.74 ounces, 20g) cornstarch

1 teaspoon ground cinnamon

1 egg white, beaten, for egg wash

1. In a bowl, combine the sliced apples with ½ cup of sugar and the salt. Adjust the sugar based on how sweet your apples are. Set the apples aside to macerate for 1 to 2 hours.

2. Roll out half of the pie dough to about a 12-inch circle and fit it into a 9-inch deep-dish pie plate. Roll the other half of dough to a 12-inch circle. Sprinkle with flour, fold in half, then fold again. Wrap in plastic and set into the dough-lined pie plate. Set the pie plate in the refrigerator.

3. Preheat the oven to 350°F. Drain the apples, reserving the juice. In a small container, mix ¼ cup of the reserved juice with the cornstarch.

4. In a small saucepan, heat the remaining juice on medium-high until it begins to boil. Reduce the heat to low and whisk in the cornstarch slurry. Return to a boil, whisking constantly, until the juice is thickened and becomes translucent. Immediately toss the thickened juice and the cinnamon in the bowl with the apple slices.

Continued

5. Remove the pie plate from the refrigerator, setting aside the wrapped crust, and pour the apples into the pie plate. Brush the edges of the bottom crust with some of the egg white. Unwrap and unfold the dough for the top crust and lay it over the filling. Pinch the two crusts together to seal, then trim the excess so there is 1 inch of overhang all the way around. Use a fork or your fingers to crimp the crust.

6. Brush the entire top of the pie with egg white and sprinkle generously with granulated sugar. Use a knife to cut a steam vent in the middle of the pie.

7. Place the pie on a baking sheet and bake for about 1 hour, or until the crust is golden brown and the fruit in the middle of the pie is tender. Serve slightly warm or at room temperature.

BAKING SCIENCE TIP: Macerating the apples with sugar will help the fruit keep its shape while baking. When fruit is cooked, the cell walls weaken and the water in the fruit leaks out. The fruit loses its structure and becomes mushy. That's how applesauce is made. When uncooked fruit is tossed with sugar, the sugar is drawn into the fruit and reinforces the cell walls, allowing the fruit to maintain its shape while baking. Precooking the starch with the juice ensures that the starch is activated so the filling will never be runny!

APPLE-CINNAMON GALETTE

Serves 8

Whoever coined the phrase "easy as pie" was probably making a galette. A galette is a free-form tart that's made by rolling your dough into a rough circle and simply folding it around the filling. A galette is supposed to look rustic, so this is a no-fuss, no-muss recipe. NUT-FREE

PREP TIME: 10 minutes

BAKE TIME: 20 to 25 minutes

EQUIPMENT: Baking sheet, parchment paper or silicone baking mat, rolling pin, mixing bowls, pastry brush

½ recipe Flaky Pie Dough (page 113)

¼ cup dry bread crumbs

2 pounds (about 5 medium) apples, cored, peeled, halved, and sliced ¼ inch thick

¼ cup (2 ounces, 55g) granulated sugar

1 teaspoon ground cinnamon

1 egg, beaten, for egg wash

Demerara or granulated sugar, for sprinkling

1. Preheat the oven to 400°F. Line a baking sheet with parchment paper or a silicone baking mat.

2. Roll the dough to a 16-inch round, about ¼ inch thick. Transfer the dough to the prepared baking sheet. Sprinkle the bread crumbs over the dough, leaving a 1-inch border around the edges. Arrange the apples over the bread crumbs. In a bowl, combine the granulated sugar with the cinnamon and sprinkle over the apples. Fold the 1-inch border of dough over the apples, creating a stuffed crust.

3. Brush the border with the egg wash and sprinkle with Demerara sugar.

4. Bake for 20 to 25 minutes, or until the apples are tender and the crust is well browned.

5. Enjoy warm or at room temperature.

BAKING TIP: If you own a pizza stone, you'll want to use it for this recipe. Preheat the stone for a least an hour. Slide the assembled galette directly onto the stone and bake as directed.

STRAWBERRY HAND PIES

⇒ *Makes 18 pies* ⇐

Hand pies are perfect little pockets of deliciousness. This recipe is extra simple because the pies are filled with premade strawberry preserves. You can fill the pies with any preserve or jam, or with your favorite chocolate hazelnut spread. NUT-FREE

- -

PREP TIME: 30 minutes, plus 30 minutes to chill

BAKE TIME: 15 minutes

EQUIPMENT: Rolling pin, round cookie cutter, baking sheet, parchment paper, mixing bowl, whisk, pastry brush

1 recipe Cream Cheese Pie Dough (page 114)
1 egg
Pinch salt
1 (12-ounce) jar strawberry preserves
Sugar, for sprinkling

TECHNIQUE TIP: To make the process even simpler, cut the dough into 4-by-8-inch rectangles, brush egg wash on the edges, fill, and fold each rectangle over to form a 4-inch square.

1. Roll out the dough ⅛ inch thick. Use a 3- or 3½-inch round cookie cutter or the rim of a glass to cut the dough into circles. Place the circles on a parchment paper–lined baking sheet, stacking them if necessary, with a sheet of parchment between each layer. Piece together the dough scraps, re-roll, and cut until all the dough is used. Cover with plastic wrap and refrigerate for 30 minutes.

2. Preheat the oven to 375°F. Whisk the egg with the salt to make an egg wash. Lay half of the chilled dough rounds on a work surface. Brush the entire surface of the rounds with the egg wash. Spoon a generous tablespoon of preserves onto each round. Place the remaining rounds on top of the filling. Pinch together the edges of each pie, making sure they are well sealed.

3. Place the filled pies on the same parchment-lined baking sheet used in step 1. Use a fork to poke vent holes on the top of each pie. Brush the pies with the egg wash and sprinkle with the sugar.

4. Bake for about 15 minutes, or until puffed and golden brown. The pies can be enjoyed warm or at room temperature.

BANANA CREAM PIE

Serves 8

This recipe may look a little complicated, with lots of ingredients and steps, but it's really quite easy to put together. Banana cream pie is great the day it's made, but it's even better the next day, after the flavors meld and the bananas soften into the filling. It's the perfect make-ahead dessert. NUT-FREE

PREP TIME: 40 minutes, plus 30 minutes to chill

BAKE TIME: 15 minutes

EQUIPMENT: 9-inch pie plate, mixing bowls, saucepan, whisk, mesh sieve, electric mixer

FOR THE CRUST

1½ cups (8 ounces, 224g) graham cracker crumbs (about 14 crackers)

¼ cup (2 ounces, 56g) granulated sugar

6 tablespoons (3 ounces, 85g) unsalted butter, melted

4 ounces (112g) semisweet chocolate, finely chopped

FOR THE BANANA PASTRY CREAM AND TOPPING

1½ cups (12 ounces, 360 ml) whole milk

½ vanilla bean, split lengthwise, seeds scraped, and pod reserved, or 1 teaspoon vanilla extract

½ cup plus 2 tablespoons (5 ounces, 140g) granulated sugar

Pinch salt

2 large eggs plus 2 large yolks

3 tablespoons (1.1 ounces, 30g) cornstarch

3 tablespoons unsalted butter

2 tablespoons rum (optional)

3 large or 4 medium ripe bananas, cut into ½-inch-thick slices

FOR ASSEMBLING THE PIE

2 cups (1 pint, 480 ml) heavy cream

3 tablespoons confectioners' sugar

2 teaspoons dark rum (optional)

Chocolate curls or chocolate chips (optional)

Continued

TO MAKE THE CRUST

1. Preheat the oven to 350°F. In a bowl, combine the graham cracker crumbs and sugar. Sprinkle the melted butter over the crumbs and toss to combine. Press the crumbs into the bottom and up the side of a 9-inch pie plate. Bake for 10 to 15 minutes, or until golden brown and fragrant.

2. While the crust is still warm, sprinkle the chopped chocolate into the bottom of the pie shell. Allow the chocolate to melt, then gently spread it across the bottom and side of the pie shell. Set the crust aside to cool while you make the filling.

TO MAKE THE BANANA PASTRY CREAM AND TOPPING

1. Pour the milk into a medium saucepan. Add the vanilla bean seeds and pod to the milk. Warm over medium-high heat until scalding hot.

2. Meanwhile, in a large bowl, whisk together the sugar, salt, whole eggs, egg yolks, and cornstarch until smooth. When the milk is scalding hot, whisk it into the egg mixture. Return the custard to the saucepan and cook over medium-low heat, stirring constantly, until it just it begins to boil. Remove from the heat and use a sieve to strain the custard back into the bowl. Add the butter and rum (if using) to the hot custard and whisk to combine. Fold the banana slices into the pastry cream. Cover with plastic wrap and refrigerate until cold.

TO ASSEMBLE THE PIE

Pour the cooled banana cream into the pie shell and smooth to an even layer. Using an electric mixer, whip the cream with the confectioners' sugar and rum (if using). Spread the whipped cream over the filling. Decorate the pie with chocolate curls or chocolate chips, if desired.

INGREDIENT TIP: The rum is optional in both the filling and the cream. It doesn't make the pie taste "boozy," but it does enhance the other flavors. Leftover egg whites can be frozen for up to a month. Let the frozen whites thaw and use in any recipe that calls for egg whites. Chocolate chips can be substituted for the semisweet chocolate.

BLUEBERRY-VANILLA BUTTERMILK PIE

⇒ Serves 8 ⇐

Originally from Britain but very popular in the southern United States, buttermilk pie is an old-fashioned recipe that deserves renewed attention. The special flavor of buttermilk custard marries perfectly with the sweet blueberries in this filling. And what could be easier than simply mixing all the ingredients together and baking? NUT-FREE

PREP TIME: 30 minutes

BAKE TIME: 45 minutes

EQUIPMENT: Rolling pin, 9-inch pie plate, baking sheet, mixing bowl, whisk

½ recipe Flaky Pie Dough (page 113)

1 cup (8 ounces, 224g) granulated sugar

¼ cup (1.5 ounces, 40g) cornstarch

¼ teaspoon salt

2 large eggs plus 2 yolks

1½ cups (12 ounces, 360 ml) buttermilk

½ cup (4 ounces, 120 ml) heavy cream

2 tablespoons (1 ounce, 30g) unsalted butter, melted

Seeds from ½ vanilla bean or 2 teaspoons vanilla extract

2 pints fresh or frozen blueberries

INGREDIENT TIP: If you're using frozen blueberries, leave them in the freezer until you're ready to put them into the piecrust. The pie may take a few minutes longer to bake with the frozen berries.

1. Roll the dough and fit it into the bottom and up the side of a 9-inch pie plate. Trim and crimp the edge. Refrigerate while you prepare the filling.

2. Preheat the oven to 350°F. Place a baking sheet on the bottom rack to preheat.

3. Whisk together the sugar, cornstarch, and salt. Add the whole eggs and egg yolks and whisk until smooth. Whisk in the buttermilk, cream, melted butter, and vanilla bean seeds.

4. Remove the piecrust from the refrigerator. Pull out the bottom oven shelf and set the piecrust on the preheated baking sheet. Spread the berries in the crust and pour the custard over the berries.

5. Bake for 15 minutes, then reduce the oven temperature to 325°F. Continue baking until the custard is set, about another 30 minutes.

6. Cool on a wire rack to room temperature. Serve at room temperature or chilled. Leftovers should be refrigerated.

LEMON MERINGUE PIE

Serves 8

Is there anything prettier than a slice of lemon meringue pie? I don't think so. A flaky piecrust filled with zesty filling and topped with billowy, toasty meringue is a thing of beauty. Add to that a flavor that enlivens the taste buds, and you've got a classic recipe for the ages. NUT-FREE

PREP TIME: 1 hour

BAKE TIME: 1 hour

EQUIPMENT: Rolling pin, 9-inch pie plate, aluminum foil, baking sheet, pastry brush, saucepan, whisk, mixing bowl, electric mixer, rasp grater

FOR THE CRUST

½ recipe Flaky Pie Dough (page 113)
1 egg white, beaten, for egg wash

FOR THE FILLING

¼ cup plus 2 tablespoons (2.2 ounces, 61.5g) cornstarch
1⅓ cups (11 ounces, 308g) granulated sugar
2 cups (16 ounces, 480 ml) water
¼ teaspoon salt
8 egg yolks
Finely grated zest of 1 lemon
⅔ cup (6 ounces, 180 ml) freshly squeezed lemon juice
3 tablespoons (1.5 ounces, 42g) unsalted butter

FOR THE MERINGUE

1 tablespoon (.37 ounces, 10g) cornstarch
⅓ cup (3 ounces, 90 ml) water
5 egg whites
¼ teaspoon cream of tartar
½ cup (4 ounces, 112g) granulated sugar

TO MAKE THE CRUST

1. Roll the dough to fit the bottom and side of a 9-inch pie plate. Crimp the edge and use a fork to prick the bottom of the crust all over. Chill for at least 30 minutes.

2. Preheat the oven to 350°F. Line the chilled dough with aluminum foil, coming up over the edge of the pie plate to prevent the crust from burning. Fill with pie weights, dried beans, or sugar. Set on a baking sheet and bake on the lowest rack of the oven for 45 to 55 minutes, or until the crust is golden brown. Remove from the oven. Remove the foil and weights. Immediately brush the entire inside of the crust with the egg white wash. Set aside. Reduce the oven temperature to 325°F.

TO MAKE THE FILLING

1. In a large saucepan, whisk together the cornstarch, sugar, water, and salt. Cook over medium heat, stirring often, until the mixture comes to a simmer. Stir constantly until the mixture thickens to a pudding-like consistency and becomes translucent. Remove from the heat.

2. Whisk in the egg yolks, lemon zest, lemon juice, and butter. Return to the heat and bring the mixture back to a simmer, stirring constantly. Pour the hot filling into the crust. Immediately make the meringue.

TO MAKE THE MERINGUE AND FINISH THE PIE

1. In a small saucepan, bring the cornstarch and water to a simmer. Cook, stirring constantly, until the mixture thickens to a pudding-like consistency and becomes translucent. Transfer to a small bowl to cool.

2. In a large bowl, using an electric mixer, whip the egg whites with the cream of tartar until foamy. Slowly add the sugar and whip to soft peaks. Add the cornstarch mixture and whip to full peaks.

3. Gently dollop the meringue onto the filling in the piecrust, being careful not to let it sink into the filling. Mound the meringue so it's higher in the middle than on the side. Use a small offset spatula or the back of a spoon to make attractive swirls and peaks in the meringue.

4. Set the pie, still on the baking sheet, in the oven and bake for about 15 minutes, or until the meringue is golden brown.

5. Let the pie cool completely before serving. It will keep at room temperature for a day. Refrigerate leftovers.

TECHNIQUE TIP: To make a quick meringue, skip the cornstarch and water and just whip the whites with the cream of tartar and sugar. Bake as directed. This meringue will not hold up as well, so the pie should be served shortly after it is made.

CHOCOLATE TRUFFLE TART

⋛ Serves 12 ⋚

This is a sleek and sexy dessert. One look at a slice of this tart and you know all your chocolate cravings will be satisfied. You can top the tart with whipped cream or just serve it with a sprinkle of confectioners' sugar and a scoop of ice cream on the side. It's also wonderful with fresh raspberries or strawberries. NUT-FREE

PREP TIME: 45 minutes
BAKE TIME: 20 to 25 minutes
EQUIPMENT: 10- or 12-inch fluted tart pan, rolling pin, microwave-safe bowl, whisk, mixing bowl

1 recipe Chocolate Short Dough (page 116)
8 ounces (225g) bittersweet chocolate, chopped
4 tablespoons (2 ounces, 60g) unsalted butter
½ cup (4 ounces, 112g) sour cream, at room temperature
½ teaspoon vanilla extract
¼ teaspoon salt
5 large eggs
½ cup (4 ounces, 112g) granulated sugar
Whipped cream or ice cream, for serving

1. Preheat the oven to 350°F. Roll the dough to line a 10- or 12-inch fluted tart pan with a removable bottom. Transfer to the refrigerator to chill for 15 minutes. Use a fork and prick the bottom of the crust all over. Bake for 10 minutes, or until the tart shell is set. Remove from the oven and set aside while you make the filling.

2. Reduce the oven temperature to 325°F. Place the chocolate and butter in a microwave-safe bowl. Heat in 30-second increments, stirring in between, until all the chocolate is melted. Stir in the sour cream, vanilla, and salt, mixing until the mixture is smooth.

3. In a mixing bowl, add the eggs and sugar. Set the bowl over a pot of simmering water. Whisk until the mixture is warm to the touch. Remove from the heat and whisk the eggs until they triple in volume, become lighter, and leave a trail on the surface as you're mixing.

4. Whisk one-quarter of the egg mixture into the chocolate base until smooth. Fold in the remaining egg mixture in two batches. Continue folding in until all of the egg mixture is incorporated and the texture is smooth.

5. Pour the batter into the tart shell. Bake for 13 to 15 minutes, or until the filling is set in the center.

6. Transfer the tart to a wire rack and let cool to room temperature. Lift the bottom of the pan out of the rim. Serve the tart at room temperature or slightly chilled, with a dollop of whipped cream or a scoop of ice cream.

TECHNIQUE TIP: For the filling of this tart, you will "ribbon" the eggs with the sugar. This involves whisking the eggs with the sugar until they aerate and lighten in color. When you lift the whisk and drizzle the eggs back into the bowl, they'll leave a ribbon print on the surface.

DUTCH APPLE TART

⇒ Serves 12 ⇐

This apple tart has a cookie-type crust and is baked in
a springform pan or cake pan. The filling is simply good
old-fashioned apples tossed with sugar, bread crumbs, and a
little cinnamon. There is no thickener in the filling, so the juices get
reabsorbed by the apples and the crust as it cools. NUT-FREE

PREP TIME: 45 minutes

BAKE TIME: 1 hour 15 minutes

EQUIPMENT: 9-inch springform pan or
round cake pan, mixing bowl, electric
mixer (optional), rasp grater, pastry
brush, pizza cutter (optional)

FOR THE DOUGH

3 cups (15 ounces, 425g)
    all-purpose flour
½ cup (4 ounces, 112g) granulated sugar
½ cup (4 ounces, 112g) packed
    brown sugar
½ teaspoon salt
Very finely grated zest of 1 lemon
2½ sticks (10 ounces, 280g) unsalted
    butter, at room temperature
1 large egg, beaten

FOR THE FILLING

3 pounds apples, cored, peeled, and cut
    into quarters
½ cup plus 2 tablespoons (5 ounces,
    140g) granulated sugar, plus more for
    sprinkling
½ teaspoon ground cinnamon
¼ cup dry bread crumbs
1 egg, beaten, for egg wash

TO MAKE THE DOUGH

1. Preheat the oven to 325°F. Liberally
butter a 9-inch springform pan or round
cake pan.

2. In a large bowl, add the flour, granulated
sugar, brown sugar, salt, and lemon zest.
Using an electric mixer or a wooden spoon,
mix the butter into the dry ingredients until
thoroughly combined. Add the egg and mix
until wet crumbs form.

3. Reserve and refrigerate one-third of the
dough for the top of the tart. Sprinkle the
remaining dough into the pan and press
the crumbs into an even layer to cover the
bottom and side of the pan, making sure
there are no gaps in the dough.

TO MAKE THE FILLING AND
ASSEMBLE THE TART

1. Cut each apple quarter into ¼-inch-thick
slices and toss with the granulated sugar
and cinnamon. Spread the bread crumbs
in the bottom of the tart shell, then pour the
apples over the bread crumbs. The pan will
be two-thirds to three-quarters full. Brush
the inside of the tart shell, from the apples
to the top, with egg wash.

2. Remove the reserved one-third of dough from the refrigerator and roll into a 10-inch round. Use a pizza cutter or sharp knife to cut the dough into 1-inch strips. Arrange the strips in a lattice pattern over the apples. If a strip breaks, just pinch it back together. Trim the excess dough, brush the top with egg wash, and sprinkle with granulated sugar.

3. Bake the tart for about 1 hour and 15 minutes, or until the apples in the middle are tender and the juices are bubbling. Transfer to a wire rack and let cool to room temperature in the pan. To unmold the tart, run a thin knife around the edge to unstick the tart, then release the springform pan. If you are using a cake pan, run the knife around the edge, then place a plate on top of the tart and flip it over onto a serving platter, then flip it right-side up.

INGREDIENT TIP: I like to use tart apples for this filling. Granny Smiths are widely available and a good option. Depending on how sweet your apples are, you might need to adjust the amount of sugar in the filling to suit your taste. Also, the exact baking time will vary based on how firm the apples are.

TARTE TATIN

Serves 8

A classic tarte Tatin is absolutely perfect in its simplicity. What could be lovelier than a flaky crust topped with buttery, caramelized apples? And when I say buttery, I mean buttery. Many tarte Tatin recipes use puff pastry for the crust. I prefer Flaky Pie Dough (page 113) because it's more substantial and can hold up under the apples and caramel. However, you can certainly use puff pastry if that's your preference. NUT-FREE

PREP TIME: 20 minutes

COOK TIME: 15 to 20 minutes

BAKE TIME: 20 to 25 minutes

EQUIPMENT: Rolling pin, cast iron skillet

½ recipe Flaky Pie Dough (page 113)

1 stick (4 ounces, 112g) unsalted butter

¾ cup (6 ounces, 168g) granulated sugar

¼ teaspoon salt

3 pounds apples, cored, peeled, and cut into quarters

1. Roll the pie dough to a 12-inch round, or a little larger than your skillet. Fold the dough in quarters, wrap in plastic, and refrigerate.

2. Preheat the oven to 375°F. Heat a 9- or 10-inch cast iron skillet on medium-high.

3. Melt the butter in the skillet. Add the sugar and salt, stirring to combine. Continue cooking, stirring frequently, until the sugar begins to melt and caramelize. When all the sugar is melted and the caramel is a light amber color, remove the pan from the heat.

4. Beginning at the outside edge of the pan, lay the apples on their sides in concentric circles, packing them in as tightly as you can so they can remain upright as they cook. Reserve any apples that don't fit into the pan.

5. Cook over medium heat for about 10 minutes, or until the apples have shrunk a bit and are well browned on the bottom. Flip them with a fork and fit any reserved apples in the pan. Cook until the apples are still slightly firm in the center and are well browned on both sides.

6. Remove the pan from the heat and let the apples cool to room temperature.

7. Unfold the pie dough and lay it over the apples. Tuck the edges of the dough between the apples and the pan.

8. Transfer the skillet to the oven and bake for 20 to 25 minutes, until the crust is golden brown.

9. Remove the skillet from the oven and let cool for 15 to 20 minutes. Place a large platter over the skillet and quickly flip the entire thing. Remove the skillet. If any apples stick to the skillet, lift them off and place them on the tart. Serve warm.

MAKE-AHEAD TIP: You can bake the tart several hours before serving. Leave it in the skillet. Before serving, reheat in the oven or on the stove top.

FRESH FRUIT TART

This tart will surely impress your guests. Each of the components can be made ahead, so it's a low-stress recipe to put together when you're entertaining. A light coating of apricot preserves gives the fresh fruit a glistening finish. Sit back and enjoy the compliments! NUT-FREE

PREP TIME: 30 minutes, plus 1 hour 30 minutes to chill

BAKE TIME: 15 minutes

EQUIPMENT: 10- or 12-inch fluted tart pan, microwave-safe bowl, mesh sieve, pastry brush

1 recipe Short Dough (page 115)

4 ounces (115g) semisweet chocolate, finely chopped

1 recipe Vanilla Pastry Cream (page 141), freshly made

About 4 cups seasonal fresh berries and sliced fruit

1 cup (12 ounces, 340g) apricot preserves

1. Roll the dough to fit a 10- or 12-inch fluted tart pan with a removable bottom. Refrigerate for 30 minutes.

2. Preheat the oven to 375°F. Remove the tart shell from the refrigerator and use a fork to prick the bottom 6 to 8 times.

3. Bake for about 15 minutes, or until the tart shell is golden brown. As soon as it comes out of the oven, sprinkle the chopped chocolate into the bottom of the shell. Let the chocolate melt, then spread evenly in the shell. Set aside to cool completely.

4. Make the pastry cream according to the recipe, and pour the still-warm pastry cream into the tart shell. Spread the cream into an even layer, lay plastic wrap directly on the surface, and transfer it to the refrigerator to chill completely, at least 1 hour.

5. When the tart is chilled, remove from the refrigerator, remove the plastic wrap, and arrange fresh berries and/or sliced fresh fruit in an attractive pattern on top of the pastry cream. Use enough fruit to completely cover the surface of the tart.

6. Put the apricot preserves in a microwave-safe bowl and heat in the microwave until soft enough to strain through a mesh sieve. Brush the warm preserves all over the fruit.

7. Serve the tart chilled.

TECHNIQUE TIP: Lining the tart shell with chocolate adds a wonderful flavor, but it also prevents the pastry cream from seeping into the crust and making it soggy.

BLUEBERRY COBBLER IN A CAST IRON SKILLET

> ≳ *Serves 8* ≲

I love the combination of cornbread and blueberries. The two flavors come together perfectly in this wonderful, homey dish. Absolutely no special baking skills are needed for this cobbler. Simply present it at the table right in the cast iron skillet. A serving of this cobbler just begs for a scoop of vanilla ice cream on the side. NUT-FREE

PREP TIME: 15 minutes

BAKE TIME: 35 to 40 minutes

EQUIPMENT: Cast iron skillet or casserole dish, mixing bowls, whisk, rasp grater, baking sheet, aluminum foil

6 tablespoons (3 oz, 84g) unsalted butter
6 cups (3 pints, 850g) blueberries
⅔ cup (2.5 ounces, 70g) granulated sugar, divided
¼ teaspoon salt, plus pinch
Finely grated zest and juice of 1 lemon
⅔ cup (2.5 ounces, 70g) cornmeal
½ cup (2.5 ounces, 70g) all-purpose flour
2 teaspoons baking powder
½ teaspoon ground cinnamon
½ cup (4 ounces, 120 ml) buttermilk
1 egg

1. Preheat the oven to 375°F.

2. Set a 9- or 10-inch cast iron skillet over low heat and melt the butter in it. Swirl the pan to coat the bottom and side. Pour ¼ cup of the butter out of the pan and set aside.

3. In a medium bowl, mix together the blueberries, ⅓ cup of sugar, a pinch of salt, and the lemon zest and juice. Pour the berry mixture into the skillet.

4. In the same bowl, whisk together the cornmeal, flour, remaining ⅓ cup of sugar, the baking powder, cinnamon, and remaining ¼ teaspoon of salt. In a separate bowl, combine the buttermilk, reserved melted butter, and egg. Make a well in the center of the dry ingredients and pour in the buttermilk mixture. Stir just until combined.

5. Drop dollops of the batter all over the berries in the skillet, spreading the batter to cover the berries as much as possible. Some berries may be visible. Slide a sheet pan lined with aluminum foil on the shelf beneath where the cobbler will bake in the oven to catch any drips.

6. Transfer the skillet to the oven and bake for 35 to 40 minutes, or until the topping is golden brown and the berries are bubbling.

7. Serve the cobbler warm or at room temperature.

SUBSTITUTION TIP: If you don't have a cast iron skillet, you can bake the cobbler in a casserole dish brushed with melted butter.

CHURROS *page 142*

Chapter 6
CROISSANTS & PASTRIES

QUICK TUTORIAL

About Pastry

We often refer to almost any sweet treat as a pastry. But when is something truly a pastry, as opposed to a cookie, cake, or pie? Here's my take: When the dough is the defining characteristic of a dish, I call it a pastry. Unlike a tart or pie, which is mostly defined by what's in the shell, a pastry is really defined by the type of dough used to make it.

Helpful Hints

◆ The two biggest concerns when working with pastry doughs are temperature and gluten. The best way to control the temperature and the gluten in a dough is to chill and rest the dough as you work.

◆ Many of these doughs get their particular texture from the way the fat is dispersed. This is especially true of laminated dough. What is a laminated dough? In the traditional technique, laminating happens when the dough is wrapped around a block of butter. The dough is then rolled, folded, and "turned" a total of six times over several hours.

◆ As a laminated dough bakes, the water in it creates steam, and the dough rises. As the dough rises, the layers of butter keep the sheets of dough separated. The result is a dough with hundreds of distinct layers that rise tall in the heat of the oven. This is what I mean by science in baking!

Shortcuts/Time-Savers

◆ In this book, I use one shortcut technique for all three laminated dough recipes: puff pastry, croissant, and Danish.

◆ Quick puff pastry is made by mixing chunks of butter into the dough, then doing a few quick folds to create the layers. Puff pastry made with the "quick" method doesn't have quite as many layers as traditional puff pastry. But the trade-off is well worth it since this shortcut will save you hours in the kitchen. The entire mixing, rolling, and folding process takes only 15 to 20 minutes.

◆ Croissant and Danish are similar to puff pastry, but their doughs have yeast, sugar, and other ingredients added to enrich them.

◆ I always make more dough than I need and store extras in the freezer for later.

◆ Of course, the ultimate shortcut is to buy prepackaged frozen dough. Puff pastry and phyllo dough are two of the best premade dough products available. Don't feel like you're cheating—I have seen both used in many professional kitchens and have used them myself.

CREAM PUFFS (PATE A CHOUX)

Makes 12 puffs

This classic pastry recipe provides the base for many desserts, including cream puffs. The puffs can be filled with vanilla cream filling, or you can fill them with ice cream to make profiteroles. The same batter can be piped into oblong strips to make éclairs. NUT-FREE

PREP TIME: 30 minutes

BAKE TIME: 30 minutes

EQUIPMENT: Baking sheets, parchment paper or silicone baking mats, saucepan, whisk, food processor (optional), cookie scoop (optional), piping bag (optional)

FOR THE PUFFS

1 cup (8 ounces, 240 ml) water
4 tablespoons (2 ounces, 56g) unsalted butter
1 teaspoon granulated sugar
¼ teaspoon salt
1 cup (5 ounces, 140g) all-purpose flour
3 large eggs plus 2 whites, at room temperature

FOR THE FILLING

1 cup (8 ounces, 240 ml) heavy cream
¼ cup (1 ounce, 28g) confectioners' sugar, plus more for sprinkling
1 recipe Vanilla Pastry Cream (page 141), chilled (see Tip)

TO MAKE THE PUFFS

1. Preheat the oven to 400°F. Line a baking pan with parchment paper or a silicone baking mat. If using parchment paper, place a dab of batter into the four corners of the pan to stick the parchment to the pan.

2. In a small saucepan, combine the water, butter, granulated sugar, and salt. Bring the water to a full boil. Remove the pan from the heat and add the flour all at once. Vigorously stir the batter until the flour is absorbed and there are no lumps. Return the pan to medium-low heat and continue stirring for 3 minutes. The batter will come together and form a smooth, cohesive ball.

3. Remove the pan from the heat and transfer the batter to a food processor fitted with a blade. If mixing by hand, transfer to a large bowl. In a separate bowl, whisk the whole eggs and egg whites together. With the processor running, add the eggs in a steady stream. Process until the batter comes together. If mixing by hand, add the eggs in three batches. After each addition, stir vigorously until the batter comes together.

Continued

4. Use a cookie scoop or tablespoon to scoop 12 mounds of batter onto the prepared baking sheet, about 2 inches apart. Use wet fingertips to tamp down any points and shape the batter into smooth rounds. Bake for about 20 minutes, until nicely puffed and golden brown.

5. Remove the puffs from the oven and turn off the heat. Use a paring knife to form a small hole in the bottom of each puff. Return the baking sheet to the still-warm oven and allow the puffs to dry for at least 30 minutes.

6. Let the puffs cool to room temperature before filling.

TO FILL THE CREAM PUFFS

1. Whip the cream with the confectioners' sugar. Fold the whipped cream into the pastry cream in two batches. Don't over-stir.

2. Scoop the cream into a pastry bag fitted with a small plain tip. Pipe the filling into the hole at the bottom of the puff. If you don't have a piping bag, you can snip the corner off of a resealable plastic bag. Alternatively, slice off the top third of the puff and spoon the filling in, then replace the tops. Refrigerate until ready to serve. Sprinkle with confectioners' sugar just before serving.

MAKE-AHEAD TIP: The unfilled baked puffs freeze very well. Gently pack them into freezer bags and freeze for up to a month. When you're ready to fill them, line the frozen puffs on a baking pan and heat in a 350°F oven for 5 minutes. Let cool, then fill. Also, use the egg yolks that have been separated from the egg whites for this recipe in your Vanilla Pastry Cream (see page 141).

VANILLA PASTRY CREAM

Makes 1 ½ cups

This pastry cream is a classic partner for your pastry. Use it to fill cream puffs or éclairs. Add some chocolate or bananas to make a delicious cream pie filling. Spread it under fresh fruit in a tart shell, or between layers of puff pastry for napoleons. This one recipe has many uses. NUT-FREE

PREP TIME: 10 minutes, plus 2 hours to chill
COOK TIME: 5 minutes
EQUIPMENT: Saucepan, heatproof bowl, whisk, mesh sieve, wax or parchment paper

1 cup (8 ounces, 240 ml) whole milk
⅓ cup (3 ounces, 84g) granulated sugar, divided
Pinch salt
½ vanilla bean, split lengthwise, seeds scraped, and pod reserved, or 2 teaspoons vanilla extract
1 large egg plus 2 large yolks
2 tablespoons (.74 ounce, 20g) cornstarch
2 tablespoons (1 ounce, 25g) unsalted butter, at room temperature
2 teaspoons (.33 ounce, 10g) dark rum (optional)

1. In a medium saucepan, heat the milk, half of the sugar, the salt, and the vanilla bean seeds and pod until scalding. Meanwhile, in a large heatproof bowl, whisk together the whole egg, egg yolks, remaining sugar, and cornstarch until smooth.

2. Whisk the scalding milk into the egg mixture, then return the custard to the pan. Cook over low heat, stirring constantly, until the mixture thickens and just begins to boil.

3. Immediately strain the pastry cream into a clean bowl. Add the butter and rum (if using). Stir until the butter is melted. Cover the surface of the cream with wax paper or buttered parchment paper and let cool to room temperature. Refrigerate for at least 2 hours or overnight until completely cooled and set.

VARIATION TIP: To make chocolate pastry cream, add 4 ounces of chopped semisweet chocolate along with the butter and stir until the chocolate is melted. To make coffee-flavored pastry cream, add 1 tablespoon of instant espresso powder to the milk before scalding. To make orange pastry cream, heat the zest of 1 orange along with the milk and replace the rum with Grand Marnier.

CHURROS

⇒ *Makes 16 to 24 churros* ⇐

This fried-dough recipe comes from the same type of dough used to make cream puffs and éclairs. With fewer eggs, however, the batter for churros is a little thicker than that for cream puffs. Since churros are deep-fried, they shouldn't expand quite as much as cream puffs. NUT-FREE

PREP TIME: 15 minutes

COOK TIME: 15 to 25 minutes

EQUIPMENT: Saucepans, whisk, food processor (optional), piping bag

1 cup (8 ounces, 240 ml) water

2 tablespoons (1 ounce, 30g) unsalted butter

¾ cup granulated sugar (6 ounces, 168g), plus 1 tablespoon (.5 ounce, 14g)

¼ teaspoon salt

1 cup (5 ounces, 140g) all-purpose flour

2 large eggs, at room temperature

Vegetable oil, for frying

1½ teaspoons ground cinnamon, preferably Mexican

1. In a small saucepan, combine the water, butter, 1 tablespoon of sugar, and the salt. Bring to a full boil. Remove the pan from the heat and add the flour all at once. Vigorously stir the batter until the flour is absorbed and there are no lumps. Return the pan to medium-low heat and continue stirring for 30 to 60 seconds. The batter will come together and form a smooth, cohesive ball.

2. Remove the pan from the heat and transfer the batter to a food processor fitted with a blade. If mixing by hand, transfer to a large bowl. With the processor running, add the eggs in a steady stream and process until the batter comes together. If mixing by hand, add the eggs one at a time and stir vigorously until the batter comes together. Scoop the batter into a pastry bag fitted with a large star tip. In a shallow baking dish or paper bag, mix together the remaining ¾ cup of sugar and the cinnamon.

3. In a heavy saucepan or skillet, heat 2 inches of vegetable oil to 375°F. Holding the pastry bag a couple of inches over the oil, squeeze out a 5- to 6-inch length of dough, pull it off with your fingers, and gently guide it into the oil. Pipe four or five churros at a time, being careful not to overcrowd the pan. Fry for 1 to 2 minutes, then flip and fry for another 2 to 3 minutes, or until golden brown. The exact cook time and number of churros will depend on how big they are.

4. As the churros finish cooking, remove them from the oil and roll in the cinnamon sugar. Enjoy warm. They can also be made ahead and reheated in a 200°F oven.

TECHNIQUE TIP: Using a pastry bag with a large star tip is the easiest way to make churros. If you don't have a piping bag, you can pipe the batter from a small resealable bag with the corner snipped off.

QUICK PUFF PASTRY

Makes 2 ¾ pounds

Traditional puff pastry is made by laminating the dough (see page 138). This quick version is made by mixing chunks of butter into the dough and doing a few quick folds to create layers. Puff pastry made with the "quick" method doesn't have quite as many layers as traditional puff pastry, and the layers are not perfectly even, but this shortcut saves hours in the kitchen. The entire mixing, rolling, and folding process takes just about 20 minutes! NUT-FREE

PREP TIME: 20 minutes, plus 1 hour to chill
EQUIPMENT: Mixing bowls, electric mixer (optional), pastry brush

4 sticks (16 ounces, 230g) very cold unsalted butter, cut into ½-inch cubes
4 cups (20 ounces, 570g) all-purpose flour, plus more for sprinkling
1¼ cups (10 ounces, 295 ml) cold water
1 tablespoon white vinegar
1½ teaspoons salt

1. Place the butter in a large bowl and sprinkle with a little flour, tossing to coat. In a small bowl, mix together the water, vinegar, and salt. Set aside.

2. Add the 4 cups of flour to the bowl of a stand mixer or a large mixing bowl. Add the butter cubes and run the mixer on low briefly just to distribute the butter but not to break it down. If working by hand, toss the butter cubes to mix them through the flour.

3. With the mixer on low speed, add the water all at once and mix just until the liquid is absorbed. Don't wait for the dough to come together—it should look rough and shaggy. If working by hand, stir in the water until it's mostly absorbed. Turn the dough out onto a work surface, and use your hands to grabs chunks of the dough and press together. Press the lumps together and gather the dough into a large ball (don't use a kneading motion). If the dough is still very dry and won't come together, add a teaspoon of water at a time until it comes together.

4. Use your hands to form the dough into a rough rectangle, then roll to a 12-by-16-inch rectangle. Use your hands or a scraper to straighten the edges. Fold the dough into thirds, like a letter. Gently press to flatten the rectangle a little. Brush the surface of the dough with cold water, then roll the dough up from the short side. You'll now have a short log. Press on the log to flatten it, then roll again into a 12-by-16-inch rectangle. Fold the dough into thirds again, like a letter. Press gently on the dough to flatten, and use your hands to straighten the sides.

5. Divide the dough in half and wrap each piece tightly in plastic. Let rest in the refrigerator for at least 1 hour or overnight before using. Leave the dough folded when you roll it. Wrapped tightly, the dough can be frozen for up to 3 months.

RECIPE TIP: If at any time during the process the butter begins to melt, stop and refrigerate the dough for 30 minutes to firm up the butter. This recipe makes a double batch. If you're going to the trouble of making your own puff pastry, you might as well make more for later since it freezes very well. This recipe can also be halved.

BLUEBERRY TURNOVERS

Makes 18 turnovers

This recipe is super fast, super easy, and fail-proof. By using preserves to sweeten and thicken the filling, it's not possible to end up with a filling that is undercooked. The preserves deliver sweetness, and the berries add a fresh flavor. If you can't find blueberry preserves, use apricot preserves or lemon marmalade. You can also use raspberry preserves with the blueberries to make "two-berry" turnovers. NUT-FREE

PREP TIME: 15 minutes, plus 30 minutes to chill
BAKE TIME: 10 to 15 minutes
EQUIPMENT: Baking sheets, parchment paper or silicone baking mats, mixing bowls, rolling pin, pizza cutter (optional), pastry brush

½ cup blueberry preserves
2 cups fresh or frozen blueberries
½ recipe Quick Puff Pastry (page 144)
1 egg, beaten, for egg wash
Demerara or granulated sugar, for sprinkling

SHORTCUT TIP: If you don't want to make puff pastry, you can use 2 sheets of premade frozen pastry instead. The assembled turnovers can be frozen for up to 3 months. Transfer them directly to the oven to bake—no need to let thaw.

1. Line two baking sheets with parchment paper or silicone baking mats.

2. In a large bowl, fold the preserves into the blueberries and set aside.

3. Roll the pastry to a 12-by-12-inch square, ⅜ inch thick.

4. Use a pizza cutter or sharp knife to cut the square in a 3-by-3 grid for a total of 9 squares, each about 4 inches.

5. Brush the squares with the egg wash, all the way to the edges. Place a heaping tablespoon of the blueberry filling into the center of each square. Fold the dough over the filling to form a triangle and use a fork to crimp all around the edges. Poke a vent hole on top of each turnover.

6. Place the turnovers at least 1 inch apart on the prepared baking sheets. Brush the tops with egg wash and sprinkle with sugar. Refrigerate for 30 minutes. Meanwhile, preheat the oven to 375°F.

7. Bake the turnovers for 10 to 15 minutes, or until puffed and golden brown. Serve warm or at room temperature.

PITHIVIERS

Serves 10

Choosing my favorite dessert is like choosing my favorite child: impossible. But if I had to choose, a Pithiviers would be in the running. When I tried my first slice of this shatteringly crisp puff pastry filled with rich almond frangipane, it was love at first bite. This is a classic pastry that is easy to make and very impressive.

PREP TIME: 25 minutes

BAKE TIME: 35 to 40 minutes

EQUIPMENT: Mixing bowls, electric mixer, baking sheet, parchment paper or silicone baking mat, rolling pin, pastry brush

½ cup (4 ounces, 112g) granulated sugar

4 tablespoons (2 ounces, 56g) unsalted butter, at room temperature

2 large eggs, 1 beaten for egg wash

½ cup (2 ounces, 56g) ground almonds or almond flour

¼ teaspoon salt

½ teaspoon almond extract

½ teaspoon vanilla extract

1½ teaspoons dark rum

½ recipe Quick Puff Pastry (page 144), divided in half

1. In a large mixing bowl, using an electric mixer, cream the sugar and butter together until light and fluffy. Add the whole egg and mix to combine. Add the almonds, salt, almond extract, vanilla, and rum. Refrigerate while you prepare the pastry.

2. Preheat the oven to 375°F. Line a baking sheet with parchment paper or a silicone baking mat.

3. Roll each half of the pastry to a 12-inch square, ⅜ inch thick. Use a round cake pan or the rim of a bowl to cut a 12-inch circle from each piece of dough. Save the dough scraps.

4. Place one round of dough onto the baking sheet. Brush a 2-inch border around the edges with egg wash. Spread the almond filling on the pastry, inside the egg wash border. Cut a ½-inch hole in the middle of the other pastry round. Use the tip of a sharp knife to etch arching lines from the hole at the center out toward the edge to form a pinwheel design on the top.

Continued

5. Place the top pastry round onto the filling, lining up the edges with the bottom round. Press the edges to glue the layers of dough together. Use the back of a paring knife to push around the side of the dough in 1-inch increments. This will create a scalloped pattern around the side of the Pithiviers.

6. Brush the egg wash over the entire top. Bake for 35 to 40 minutes, or until well puffed and golden brown.

7. Serve slightly warm or at room temperature.

BAKING TIP: If you don't want to make puff pastry, you can use 2 sheets of premade frozen pastry instead. To work ahead, the Pithiviers can be assembled and frozen, unbaked. Let thaw at least halfway before baking. It may need to bake a little longer. Also, the scraps of puff pastry can be gathered together and rolled in granulated sugar to make Palmiers (page 56).

CHOCOLATE & APRICOT RUGELACH

Makes 36 pieces

I just love these delicious little pastries and hope you will, too. You can find recipes for this popular Jewish pastry with all sorts of different fillings, many including dried fruits and nuts. I'm partial to the combination of tart apricot preserves and chocolate chips. The dough is very easy to work with, but it is soft and should be chilled before rolling.

PREP TIME: 1 hour, plus 1 hour to chill
BAKE TIME: 20 to 25 minutes
EQUIPMENT: Mixing bowls, electric mixer, baking sheets, parchment paper or silicone baking mats, rolling pin, pizza cutter (optional), pastry brush

2 sticks (8 ounces, 224g) unsalted butter, at room temperature
1 cup (8 ounces, 224g) cream cheese, at room temperature
⅓ cup (3 ounces, 84g) granulated sugar, plus 2 tablespoons (1 ounce, 28g)
½ teaspoon salt
2 cups (10 ounces, 280g) all-purpose flour
2 tablespoons (1 ounce, 28g) packed brown sugar
1 tablespoon ground cinnamon
¾ cup (9 ounces, 252g) apricot preserves
¾ cup (4.5 ounces, 126g) mini chocolate chips
¾ cup (3.5 ounces, 98g) ground walnuts
1 egg, beaten, for egg wash

1. Using an electric mixer on low speed, cream the butter and cream cheese until softened. Add 2 tablespoons of granulated sugar and the salt. Increase the speed to medium and cream until the mixture is light and fluffy. Reduce the speed to low, gradually add the flour, and mix until combined. Divide the dough into three equal portions. Wrap each portion in plastic and refrigerate for at least 1 hour or overnight.

2. Preheat the oven to 375°F. Line two baking sheets with parchment paper or silicone baking mats.

3. In a bowl, combine the remaining ⅓ cup of granulated sugar, the brown sugar, and cinnamon. Set aside.

Continued

4. Roll a piece of dough to a 12-inch circle, ¼ inch thick. Spread the dough round with one-third of the apricot preserves, removing any large chunks of fruit. Sprinkle with one-third of the cinnamon sugar, one-third of the chocolate chips, and one-third of the ground nuts. Press lightly on the filling to adhere it to the preserves. Using a pizza cutter or sharp knife, cut the round into 12 wedges. Roll each wedge from the wide end to the narrow end, like a croissant. Repeat with the other 2 pieces of dough.

5. Set the rugelach 1 inch apart on the prepared baking sheets. Brush the tops with the egg wash. Bake for 20 to 25 minutes, or until golden brown. Some of the apricot preserves will leak out during baking.

6. Transfer the rugelach to a wire rack and let cool completely.

MAKE-AHEAD TIP: You can make the rugelach through step 3 and freeze them for up to 3 months. Let thaw about halfway before brushing with egg wash and baking.

QUICK CROISSANTS

≥ Makes 22 croissants ≤

This recipe might look a little long for something named "quick" croissants. But this is truly a shortcut version of the classic French recipe. The dough takes just 15 minutes to mix and fold, using the same shortcut mixing method that I offer in my Quick Puff Pastry recipe (page 144). Most of the extra time is inactive, for chilling and rising the dough. If the butter becomes very soft at any point during the rolling and folding process, chill the dough for a few minutes before continuing. NUT-FREE

PREP TIME: 30 minutes,
plus 2 hours for the dough
to chill and 2 to 3 hours for it to rise
BAKE TIME: 15 to 20 minutes
EQUIPMENT: Mixing bowls, electric
mixer (optional), rolling pin, baking
sheets, parchment paper or silicone
baking mats, pizza cutter (optional),
pastry brush

½ cup (4 ounces, 120 ml) water, warmed
    to 105°F
1 packet (2¼ teaspoons, 7g)
    quick-rise yeast
3 sticks (12 ounces, 336g) cold unsalted
    butter, cut into ½-inch cubes
4 cups (20 ounces, 560g) all-purpose
    flour, plus more for sprinkling
⅓ cup (3 ounces, 84g) granulated sugar
2 teaspoons salt
1 cup (8 ounces, 240 ml) whole milk,
    slightly chilled
1 egg, beaten, for egg wash

1. In a small bowl, combine the warm water and yeast and set aside to cool to room temperature. In a separate bowl, add the butter cubes and sprinkle with a little flour. Toss to coat.

2. Place the 4 cups of flour, the sugar, and salt in the bowl of a stand mixer or a large mixing bowl. Mix for 30 seconds to distribute the ingredients. Toss in the butter cubes and run the mixer on low briefly to just distribute the butter but not to break it down. If working by hand, mix the butter through the flour just to distribute.

3. Add the milk to the water-yeast mixture. With the mixer running on low, add the liquid to the batter all at once and mix just until it is absorbed. Don't wait for the dough to come together; it should look rough and shaggy. If mixing by hand, stir the liquid in until it's mostly absorbed. Turn the dough out onto a work surface and use your hands to gather it into a ball.

Continued

4. Use your hands to form the dough into a rough rectangle, then use a rolling pin to roll to a 12-by-16-inch rectangle. Use your hands or a scraper to straighten the edges. Fold the dough into thirds, like a letter. Gently press to flatten the rectangle a little. Brush the surface of the dough with cold water, then roll the dough up from the short side. You'll now have a short log. Press on the log to flatten, then roll into a 12-by-16-inch rectangle. Fold the dough into thirds again, like a letter. Press gently on the dough to flatten, then use your hands to straighten the sides to square it off. Wrap the dough in plastic and refrigerate for at least 2 hours.

5. Line two baking sheets with parchment paper or silicone baking mats. Roll the chilled dough to a 24-by-16-inch rectangle, ¼ inch thick. With the long side facing you, fold the top half of the dough over the bottom half to form a 24-by-8-inch rectangle.

6. Starting from the left, measure along the top edge of the dough and make a mark at 2 inches. Using a pizza cutter or sharp knife, make a diagonal cut from that mark to the bottom left edge of the dough. Save the piece that you cut off.

7. Measure and mark 4-inch increments across the bottom edge of the dough from left to right. Measure and mark 4-inch increments across the top edge of the dough from left to right. You should have a pattern of one top mark between two bottom marks. Starting from the top left, make a diagonal cut from the first top mark to the second bottom mark, forming a triangle. Then cut from the second bottom mark to the second top mark. Continue this pattern to cut 10 alternating triangles.

8. Unfold the triangles and cut each in half so you have a total of 20 triangles. Unfold the smaller pieces cut from either end. Pinch them together to form a triangle. These can form two more croissants.

9. To form a croissant, hold a triangle from the wide base in one hand and gently stretch the width a little. Set the dough on the work surface, with the narrow end pointing toward you. Roll the croissant toward the pointed end, holding on to the tip and gently tugging as you roll. Bend either end of the croissant toward the middle to form a crescent shape. Set the croissants 3 inches apart on the prepared baking sheets. Brush with the egg wash and cover with plastic wrap. Set aside in

a warm spot to rise for 2 to 3 hours. The croissants will look airy and light but may not be quite doubled in size. Alternatively, refrigerate the croissants overnight and let them rise in the morning. The texture will be flakier after a night in the refrigerator, but you'll add about an hour to the rising time.

10. Preheat the oven to 375°F.

11. Bake the croissants for 15 to 20 minutes, or until golden brown. Serve warm or at room temperature.

INGREDIENT TIP: The water is warmed at the start of the recipe to activate the yeast. Make sure to allow the water-yeast mixture to cool down before adding it to the dough so you don't melt the butter. You can speed this process up a little by using a bit of your slightly chilled milk to bring the temperature of the water down just before adding it to the dough. Since the dough is kept cold, the rise time is longer, so that's why I recommend using quick-rise yeast—to speed up the rising time.

ALMOND CROISSANTS

Makes 22 croissants

These croissants filled with almond frangipane and topped with sliced almonds are a special treat. They freeze well baked or unbaked.

PREP TIME: 30 minutes, plus 2 hours for the dough to chill and 2 to 3 hours for it to rise
BAKE TIME: 15 to 20 minutes
EQUIPMENT: Mixing bowls, electric mixer, rolling pin, baking sheets, parchment paper or silicone baking mats, pizza cutter (optional), pastry brush

½ cup (4 ounces, 112g) granulated sugar
4 tablespoons (2 ounces, 56g) unsalted butter, at room temperature
1 large egg, plus 1 egg, beaten, for egg wash
½ cup (2 ounces, 56g) ground almonds or almond flour
1½ teaspoons dark rum
½ teaspoon almond extract
½ teaspoon vanilla extract
¼ teaspoon salt
1 recipe Quick Croissants (page 151)
Sliced almonds, for sprinkling

1. In a large mixing bowl, use an electric mixer to cream the sugar and butter until light and aerated. Add the large egg and mix to combine. Add the ground almonds, rum, almond extract, vanilla, and salt. Set aside.

2. Follow the steps in the Quick Croissants recipe for making and shaping the croissants. When you are ready to roll a croissant, place a tablespoon of the frangipane filling at the wide end of the triangle. Roll as directed. Brush the croissants with egg wash and sprinkle with sliced almonds. Let rise and bake as directed in the Quick Croissants recipe.

VARIATION TIP: To make chocolate croissants: Cut 20 (½-ounce) semisweet chocolate squares in half to make a total of 40 rectangles. Put two chocolate rectangles, one on top of the other, in the wide end of each croissant. Roll and bake as directed. Alternatively, a tablespoon of chocolate chips can be used.

QUICK DANISH DOUGH

Makes 2 pounds

The dough takes just 15 minutes to mix and fold. With its egg, Danish dough has a cakier texture than croissant dough. A hint of cardamom is added, if desired, for special depth of flavor. NUT-FREE

PREP TIME: 15 minutes, plus 2 hours to chill
EQUIPMENT: Mixing bowls, electric mixer (optional), rolling pin

⅓ cup (3 ounces, 90 ml) water, warmed to 105°F
1 packet (2¼ teaspoons, 7g) instant dry yeast, preferably fast-acting
2 sticks (8 ounces, 224g) cold unsalted butter, cut into ½-inch cubes
2½ cups (12.5 ounces, 350g) all-purpose flour, plus more for sprinkling
⅓ cup (3 ounces, 84g) granulated sugar
1 teaspoon salt
¼ teaspoon ground cardamom (optional)
⅓ cup (3 ounces, 90 ml) whole milk, at room temperature
1 egg, at room temperature

1. Mix the water with the yeast, then set aside to cool to room temperature. Put the butter in a bowl and sprinkle with a little flour, tossing to coat.

2. In the bowl of a stand mixer or a large mixing bowl, add the 2½ cups of flour, the sugar, salt, and cardamom (if using). Mix for 30 seconds to combine the ingredients. Add the butter cubes and mix on low speed briefly to distribute the butter but not to break it down. If mixing by hand, add the butter cubes and mix them through the flour.

3. Add the milk and egg to the water-yeast mixture. With the mixer running on low, add the milk mixture to the dry ingredients all at once, and mix just until it is absorbed. If working by hand, stir the liquid in until it's mostly absorbed. Turn the dough out onto a work surface and gather it into a large ball.

Continued

4. Use your hands to form the dough into a rough rectangle, then roll it into a 12-by-16-inch rectangle. Use your hands or a scraper to straighten the edges. Fold the dough into thirds, like a letter. Gently press to flatten the rectangle a little. Roll the dough up from the short side to make a short log. Press the log to flatten a little, then roll again into a 12-by-16-inch rectangle. Fold the dough into thirds again, like a letter. Press gently on the dough to flatten it a bit. Wrap the dough in plastic and refrigerate for at least 2 hours.

5. Use the dough immediately or freeze to use at a later date. When ready to use it, do not unfold before rolling.

VARIATION TIP: This dough is also used to make Cheese Danish Braid (page 157). To make almond Danish, you can cut the Danish dough into squares, put a dollop of Almond Croissants filling (see page 154) in the middle, fold in the four corners, pinch, and bake. To make fruit Danish, fill the squares with your favorite fruit preserves.

CHEESE DANISH BRAID

≈ Serves 12 ≈

This lovely braided pastry is quite impressive to behold, and it is the perfect dish to serve for a special brunch. To make a fresh Cheese Danish Braid for brunch, you can assemble it the evening before and simply bake it in the morning. Since it takes a few hours to rise, I set my alarm very early to take the Danish out of the refrigerator. Then I go back to bed for a few hours while the dough rises! NUT-FREE

PREP TIME: 30 minutes,
plus 2 to 3 hours for the dough to rise
BAKE TIME: 15 to 20 minutes
EQUIPMENT: Mixing bowls, electric mixer, rasp grater, rolling pin, parchment paper, pizza cutter (optional), baking sheet, pastry brush

1 cup (8 ounces, 224g) cream cheese
⅓ cup (3 ounces, 84g) granulated sugar
2 eggs, 1 beaten for egg wash
½ teaspoon finely grated lemon zest
1 teaspoon freshly squeezed lemon
   juice, plus 3 to 4 teaspoons
½ teaspoon vanilla extract
¼ teaspoon salt
1 recipe Quick Danish Dough (page 155)
¼ cup apricot preserves
½ cup (2 ounces, 56g)
   confectioners' sugar

1. In a large mixing bowl, using an electric mixer, cream the cream cheese and granulated sugar. Mix in 1 egg, the lemon zest, 1 teaspoon of lemon juice, the vanilla, and salt. Refrigerate while you prepare the dough (see page 155).

2. Turn the dough out onto a lightly floured work surface, and roll out to a 10-by-14-inch rectangle. Place the dough onto a sheet of parchment paper, with the short side of the dough facing you. Spoon the cream cheese filling into the middle of the rectangle and spread in a 3-inch-wide strip down the middle of the dough, leaving a 1-inch border at the top and bottom.

3. Using a pizza cutter or sharp knife, cut ¾-inch-wide strips in a slanting pattern on either side of the filling. Fold the top border over the filling, then "braid" the cut strips of dough by folding them into the center in a crisscross pattern going left to right, left to right, then fold the bottom border over the last strips. Use the parchment paper to slide the Danish onto a baking sheet.

Continued

4. Brush the entire braid with egg wash. Cover the braid with plastic wrap and set aside to rise for 2 to 3 hours, or place in the refrigerator overnight before rising. After rising, the dough should look light and puffy.

5. Preheat the oven to 375°F.

6. Bake the Danish for 15 to 20 minutes, or until golden brown and the filling is set. As soon as the Danish comes out of the oven, brush with the apricot preserves. Let cool for 10 minutes.

7. Meanwhile, stir together the remaining lemon juice and the confectioners' sugar. The glaze should have the texture of heavy cream. Add more sugar if it's too loose, or more lemon juice if it's too thick. Use a fork to drizzle the glaze over the Danish.

8. Serve at room temperature.

VARIATION TIP: For individual cheese Danish, cut the dough into 4-inch squares. Place a tablespoon of filling into each square. Fold the four corners into the center to cover the filling. Let rise and bake as directed.

APPLE STRUDEL

≳ Serves 12 ≲

In my first job out of pastry school, I worked for a very well-known Austrian pastry chef. I learned this recipe from him and have been making strudel with it ever since. This strudel looks huge going into the oven, but the apples cook down and the whole thing collapses a bit as you cut it into slices. You can make a smaller strudel using half the ingredients or make two smaller strudels and freeze one for later. It's the perfect dish to make for a brunch party. NUT-FREE

PREP TIME: 30 minutes

BAKE TIME: 1 hour to 1 hour 10 minutes

EQUIPMENT: Mixing bowls, rasp grater, baking sheet, parchment paper or silicone baking mat, pastry brush

½ cup (3 ounces, 85g) raisins

2½ pounds (1.13kg) apples, cored, peeled, quartered, and sliced ¼-inch thick

½ cup (4 ounces, 112g) granulated sugar

1 tablespoon freshly squeezed lemon juice

1 teaspoon finely grated lemon zest

1 teaspoon ground cinnamon

¼ teaspoon salt

1 (16-ounce) box (about 20 sheets) frozen phyllo dough, thawed

2 sticks (8 ounces, 224g) unsalted butter, melted

½ cup (1.5 ounces, 42g) dry bread crumbs

Confectioners' sugar, for sprinkling

1. Pour a cup of hot water over the raisins and set aside for 30 minutes to plump. Drain the raisins and set aside.

2. Preheat the oven to 375°F. Line a baking sheet with parchment paper or a silicone baking mat.

3. In a large bowl, add the sliced apples, sugar, lemon juice and zest, cinnamon, salt, and plumped raisins. Toss to combine.

4. Unroll the phyllo sheets and cover them with a damp towel so they don't dry out. Lay a clean kitchen towel that is larger than the baking sheet on your work surface. Lay a sheet of phyllo dough on the kitchen towel with the short side facing you. Brush the dough with melted butter, then overlap 2 more sheets of phyllo to form an 18-inch square of dough. Lay another 3 sheets of phyllo in the opposite direction, brushing each sheet with melted butter as you build the layer. Repeat, building alternating layers until all of the phyllo sheets are used.

Continued

5. Working horizontally, sprinkle the bread crumbs in a 6-inch-wide strip down the center of the pastry, leaving a 2-inch border on either end. Pour the apple filling over the bread crumbs in an even layer.

6. Starting from the side closest to you, use the kitchen towel to fold the dough over the apples. Tuck in the two ends, then continue rolling the strudel. Use the opposite side of the towel to flip the strudel so the seam side is up.

7. Use the towel to lift the strudel and gently flip it off the towel onto the baking sheet, seam-side down. Use your hands to tuck in the ends and straighten out the strudel. Brush the top of the strudel with more melted butter.

8. Bake for 1 hour to 1 hour and 10 minutes, or until the dough is deeply golden brown and the apples in the middle are tender. Poke a toothpick in the middle to see if the apples are soft. Let cool on the pan for at least 30 minutes, then transfer the strudel to a cutting board. Using a serrated knife and working on a slight angle, slice off the ragged ends of the strudel. Slice the strudel into 12 equal portions. You can remove any broken bits of phyllo to make a smoother top. Sprinkle generously with confectioners' sugar and transfer to a serving tray.

MAKE-AHEAD TIP: Make two strudels and freeze one to bake later. Allow the frozen strudel to thaw halfway before baking.

BAKLAVA

≈ Serves 18 ≈

A beautiful baklava looks very impressive, but it's deceivingly easy to make since you'll use a premade dough. The hardest part about creating this recipe is making sure that the phyllo sheets don't dry out while you're assembling the pastry.

PREP TIME: 40 minutes

BAKE TIME: 40 minutes, plus 4 hours to cool

EQUIPMENT: Food processor, rasp grater, 9-by-13-inch baking pan, pastry brush, saucepan

4 cups (16 ounces, 550g) shelled walnuts

1¼ cups (10 ounces, 283g) granulated sugar, divided

1 teaspoon ground cinnamon

¼ teaspoon ground cloves

1 (16-ounce) box (about 20 sheets) frozen phyllo dough, thawed

2 sticks (8 ounces, 224g) unsalted butter, melted

1 cup (12 ounces, 340g) honey

½ cup (4 ounces, 120 ml) water

2 tablespoons finely grated lemon zest

1 cinnamon stick

2 whole cloves

½ vanilla bean, split lengthwise, seeds scraped, and pod reserved

¼ cup (2 ounces, 60 ml) freshly squeezed lemon juice

1. Preheat the oven to 350°F.

2. In a food processor, combine the walnuts, ¼ cup of sugar, the cinnamon, and ground cloves, and grind to a coarse texture. Set aside.

3. Unroll the phyllo sheets and cover them with a damp towel so they don't dry out. Brush the bottom and sides of a 9-by-13-inch baking pan with melted butter. Lay a sheet of phyllo in the bottom of the pan, then drizzle it with melted butter. Lay another sheet of phyllo on top and drizzle with butter. Repeat with 3 more sheets of phyllo, drizzling with melted butter between every sheet.

4. Drizzle one-third of the walnut filling over the dough. Layer on another 5 phyllo sheets, drizzling with melted butter, then sprinkle with half of the remaining walnut filling. Layer on another 5 phyllo sheets, drizzling with melted butter, then sprinkle with the remaining walnut filling.

Continued

5. Finish layering the remaining phyllo sheets, drizzled with melted butter, on top of the walnut filling. Brush the entire top layer with melted butter so it doesn't dry out.

6. Use a sharp knife to cut the top section of phyllo sheets lengthwise into 6 strips, about 1½ inches wide.

7. Score the top section of strips diagonally to form diamonds. Bake for about 40 minutes, or until golden brown. Make the syrup while the pastry is baking.

8. In a small saucepan, add the honey, water, lemon zest, cinnamon stick, whole cloves, and vanilla bean seeds and pod.

Bring to a boil, reduce the heat, and simmer for 10 minutes. Add the lemon juice to the syrup, remove from the heat, and let cool. Remove the cinnamon stick, cloves, and vanilla bean pod.

9. As soon as the baklava is removed from the oven, cut through the scored lines all the way to the pan and pour the syrup over the hot baklava. Let cool at room temperature for at least 4 hours before serving.

STORAGE TIP: Baklava keeps for several days at room temperature.

CINNAMON ROLLS *page 192*

Chapter 7

YEAST BREADS

QUICK TUTORIAL

About Yeast Bread

Not surprisingly, the ingredient that defines yeast bread is the yeast. All the recipes in this book call for dry yeast. You may see dry yeast labeled as "active," "instant," or "quick-/rapid-rise." While all three of these are interchangeable, there are some differences:

◆ **Active dry yeast** has larger granules than other dry yeasts. The live yeast cells in active dry yeast are surrounded by dead yeast cells. Active dry yeast should be combined directly with a warm liquid to rehydrate and "wake up" the yeast. If you use active dry yeast in a recipe that calls for instant yeast, use 25 percent more than the amount listed in the recipe.

◆ **Instant (quick-/rapid-rise) yeast** has the smallest particles and dissolves very quickly into the dough. This type of yeast releases more carbon dioxide, and the dough will rise faster than dough made with active dry yeast. Quick-/rapid-rise yeast isn't recommended for the low- or no-knead breads since those are meant to have a long, slow rise.

The other important "ingredient" in a yeast dough is gluten. Gluten is a protein in wheat flour that creates the bread's structure. A well-developed gluten will be elastic enough to hold in the carbon dioxide bubbles formed by the yeast. If your bread dough has poorly developed gluten, the bread will tend to spread rather than rise.

Helpful Hints

◆ Yeast is a living organism that is active between about 40°F and 140°F. When working with yeast, make sure you're working within the right temperatures. Below 40°F, the yeast is still alive but becomes inactive; above 140°F, the yeast dies. A warmer dough is a more active dough, and a cooler dough will rise more slowly.

◆ There are two ways to develop gluten: kneading and waiting. Which method you use will depend on the type of dough you're working with.

◆ A technique called autolyse can be employed to allow gluten to develop naturally. Autolyse takes advantage of an enzymatic reaction in bread dough that breaks the gluten in the dough into smaller pieces. Those smaller pieces can line up and form a network more easily, allowing the gluten to develop with no or very little kneading. But all you need to know is that autolyse takes time and a very wet dough. Low-knead and no-knead breads use autolyse to skip the kneading process.

♦ A less wet dough should be kneaded, either with a dough hook on a stand mixer or by hand, to develop the gluten.

♦ **The last rise before putting bread into the oven is called "proofing."** Proof time can vary based on the temperature of the dough and of the room, so the time given in a recipe is just an estimate. To check if a loaf is ready for the oven, gently press your finger into the dough. If the dimple quickly springs back, the dough is not proofed enough. If it leaves a dimple that slowly fills in, the dough is ready for the oven.

♦ All the yeast bread recipes in this book can be made overnight to break the work up over two days. This is especially convenient if you want fresh bread for breakfast or lunch.

Shortcuts/Time-Savers

♦ Use yeast labeled "quick-rise" or "rapid-rise" for shorter rise times.

♦ A warm bread dough will rise faster than a cold or cool bread dough. To speed the rising process in a cool kitchen, you can set the bowl with your dough over a bowl of warm water. Set it up so the bottom of the bowl holding the dough doesn't touch the water. The warm water can be replaced as it cools.

♦ Because it requires no manual kneading, the process for low-knead or no-knead bread requires very little active time. Since it takes time for the dough to develop, it will take quite a few hours before your dough is ready to shape and bake, but you can go on about your business while it rises.

♦ Kneading bread dough requires more active hands-on time, but with kneading, the entire bread-making process can be finished in 2 to 3 hours.

LOW-KNEAD BREAD

Makes 1 large loaf

A "no-knead" bread recipe was originally published in the *New York Times*, and now variations of it are found all over the Internet. No-knead bread is precisely as easy as it sounds. The recipe takes more than 12 hours from start to finish, but almost all of that is hands-off time thanks to the "autolyse" technique (see page 166). I actually call this low-knead bread because you will give the dough just a few turns after the initial rise. This step takes less than a minute, but it allows us to use a little less water in the dough, making it much easier to handle than no-knead breads. DAIRY-FREE, NUT-FREE, VEGAN

PREP TIME: 10 minutes

RISE TIME: 12 to 20 hours

BAKE TIME: 55 to 60 minutes

EQUIPMENT: Mixing bowls, whisk, parchment paper, lidded oven-safe pot

3 cups (15 ounces, 360g) all-purpose flour

1½ teaspoons salt

¼ teaspoon instant dry yeast (not quick-rise)

1⅓ cups (11 ounces, 330 ml) water, at room temperature

1. In a large mixing bowl, whisk together the flour, salt, and yeast. Add the water all at once and mix with a spatula until most of the flour is incorporated. The dough will look rough and shaggy, not smooth. Cover the bowl with plastic wrap or a damp kitchen towel and let it rest at room temperature for at least 10 hours or up to 18 hours.

2. Turn the rested dough out onto a lightly floured work surface and knead very briefly, just 12 to 15 times. Pull the sides of the dough toward the center to form a round. Set the dough, seam-side down, on a sheet of parchment paper.

3. Use the parchment paper to lift the dough and set it into a heavy Dutch oven or heavy, lidded oven-safe pot. Cover the pot with plastic wrap and the lid. Leave the dough at room temperature to rise until doubled in volume, 1 hour to 1 hour and 30 minutes.

4. Remove the lid and plastic wrap from the pot. Lightly sprinkle the top of the loaf with flour and use a sharp knife, scissors, or a razor to slash a ½-inch-deep X across the top of the loaf.

5. Cover the pot and place it in the cold oven. Turn on the oven to 425°F and bake the bread for 30 minutes. Remove the lid from the pot and bake for another 25 to 30 minutes, or until the crust is deeply browned.

BAKING TIP: Yes, it is unusual to bake bread in an oven that has not been pre-heated. Most no-knead bread recipes have you preheat the Dutch oven while the oven preheats, but then you must set the dough into the hot pot. Preheating the pot speeds up the baking time; however, I prefer a less dangerous approach, even it if means a few more minutes in the oven.

FRENCH BAGUETTES

≳ Makes 2 baguette loaves ≲

True artisan bread can be a joy to make, but it takes dedication and time to learn all the intricacies of the dough. This baguette recipe, on the other hand, will yield two tasty, crusty loaves with minimal fuss. The entire process takes some time, but most of that time is hands-off. It's even easier if you let the dough rise overnight and finish baking in the morning. You'll have fresh bread by lunchtime. DAIRY-FREE, NUT-FREE, VEGAN

PREP TIME: 15 minutes
RISE TIME: 3 hours, plus overnight
to chill
BAKE TIME: 15 to 20 minutes
EQUIPMENT: Mixing bowls, electric mixer
(optional), wooden spoon or spatula,
baking sheet

1 cup (8 ounces, 240 ml) warm water
1½ teaspoons instant dry yeast
2 cups (10 ounces, 240g) all-purpose
    flour, divided
1 teaspoon salt
Cornmeal, for dusting

1. In the bowl of a stand mixer with the paddle attachment, or in a large bowl using a wooden spoon or spatula, blend the water, yeast, 1½ cups of flour, and the salt to form a thick batter.

2. If using an electric mixer, switch to the dough hook. Add the remaining ½ cup of flour, a few tablespoons at a time, until the dough gathers on the hook and begins to pull away from the side of the bowl. If mixing by hand, add the remaining flour a few tablespoons at a time until you can't mix any more. You might not use all of the flour. Turn the dough out onto a floured work surface and knead into a smooth ball.

3. Place the dough in an oiled bowl, turning once to coat. Cover the bowl with plastic wrap or a damp kitchen towel and set aside to rise in a warm place for 2 hours. Every 30 minutes, repeat the following procedure: Uncover the bowl and lift one side of the dough over into the middle of the dough. Repeat with the other three sides of the dough then flip the dough over. Cover the bowl. After 2 hours of rising and folding, refrigerate the dough overnight.

4. The next day, sprinkle a baking sheet or baguette pan generously with cornmeal. If you will bake on a baking stone, use a baking peel or the back of a baking sheet to transfer the bread to the baking stone.

5. Take the dough out of the refrigerator and, without kneading, cut it into two pieces. Gently pat each piece of dough into an 8-by-4-inch rectangle. Starting at a long side, roll the dough like a jelly roll, then use your hands to gently press the dough from the center out to form a 16-inch-long baguette. Place the two loaves side by side on the prepared baking sheet or baguette pan. Cover with a damp kitchen towel and set aside to rise at room temperature until doubled in size, about 1 hour.

6. Preheat the oven to 475°F. If using a baking stone, put it in the oven to preheat. Place a shallow pan on the bottom of the oven to preheat. Just before putting the bread in the oven, pour a cup of hot water into the shallow pan in the bottom of the oven and shut the door to capture the steam.

7. Use a very sharp knife or razor to make three diagonal slashes on top of each baguette loaf.

8. Bake for 15 to 20 minutes, or until each loaf is golden brown and sounds hollow when tapped on the bottom.

9. Transfer the loaves to a wire rack and let cool to room temperature.

SHORTCUT TIP: If you want to bake the bread on the same day you make the dough, extend the rising and folding time to 3 hours, then shape it, let rise, and bake.

MILK & HONEY WHOLE-WHEAT BREAD

Makes 1 large loaf

This bread has a soft texture, a hint of honey, and hearty whole-wheat flavor. The honey adds moisture, so the bread will stay fresh for several days. If you'd like to have fresh bread for lunch but don't want to get up before dawn to make the dough, read the make-ahead tip at the end of the recipe. NUT-FREE

PREP TIME: 40 minutes
RISE TIME: 2 to 3 hours
BAKE TIME: 30 to 35 minutes
EQUIPMENT: Mixing bowls, electric mixer (optional), wooden spoon or spatula, microwave-safe bowl, kitchen thermometer (optional), 9-by-5-inch loaf pan

½ cup (4 ounces, 120 ml) warm water
1½ cups (7.5 ounces, 210g) bread flour, divided
1 packet (2¼ teaspoons, 7g) instant dry yeast
1 cup (8 ounces, 240 ml) whole milk
2 tablespoons honey
1½ teaspoons salt
1½ cups (7.5 ounces, 210g) whole-wheat flour, preferably stone-ground
1 egg, beaten, for egg wash
Sesame seeds, for garnish (optional)

1. In the bowl of stand mixer with the paddle attachment, or in a large bowl using a wooden spoon or spatula, blend together the warm water, ½ cup of bread flour, and the yeast to form a smooth batter. Cover the bowl with plastic wrap or a damp kitchen towel and let rise for 30 minutes.

2. In a microwave-safe bowl, warm the milk in the microwave to about 100°F (if you don't have a thermometer, it's a little warmer than body temperature). Add the warmed milk, the honey, and salt to the batter in the large bowl. Mix in the whole-wheat flour and blend until the batter looks like thick pancake batter.

3. If using a stand mixer, switch to the dough hook. With the mixer running, slowly add enough of the remaining 1 cup of bread flour until the dough gathers on the hook and begins to pull away from the side of the bowl. Knead for 3-4 minutes to develop the dough. If mixing by hand, knead in enough of the remaining bread flour to form a smooth, elastic dough. You might not use all of the bread flour.

4. Turn the dough out onto a lightly floured surface and knead into a smooth ball. If the dough is very sticky, sprinkle with a little more flour as you knead. Place the dough in an oiled bowl, flip the dough to coat with oil, and cover with plastic wrap. Set the dough aside in a warm spot to rise for 1 thour to 1 hour and 30 minutes, or until doubled in size.

5. Preheat the oven to 350°F. Lightly grease a 9-by-5-inch loaf pan with vegetable oil.

6. Turn the dough out onto a floured surface and knead into a ball. Roll and push the ball from the center out toward the ends until it forms a log shape the length of the pan. Set the dough in the prepared pan and cover with oiled plastic wrap.

7. Set the dough in a warm place and let rise until it comes 1 inch over the top of the pan, 1 hour to 1 hour and 30 minutes. Use a sharp knife to cut a ½-inch-deep slash down the center of the loaf. Brush the dough with the egg wash and sprinkle with sesame seeds (if desired).

8. Bake the bread for 30 to 35 minutes, or until golden brown and a toothpick inserted in the center comes out clean.

9. Let the bread cool in the pan for 5 minutes before turning out onto a wire rack. Let cool to room temperature before slicing.

MAKE-AHEAD TIP: You can start making this bread the night before. Prepare the dough through step 5. Cover with plastic wrap and refrigerate overnight. In the morning, take the dough out and let it rise and bake as directed. The rise time may be a little longer since the dough will be cold.

WHITE SANDWICH BREAD

Makes 1 loaf (8 slices)

This is the bread you'll want to make when you're craving the perfect BLT or PB&J. It is soft and ever-so-slightly sweet—the quintessential sandwich loaf. NUT-FREE

PREP TIME: 30 minutes

RISE TIME: 2 to 3 hours

BAKE TIME: 30 to 35 minutes

EQUIPMENT: Mixing bowls, electric mixer (optional), wooden spoon or spatula, 9-by-5-inch loaf pan, pastry brush

1 cup (8 ounces, 240 ml) whole milk, warmed to 110°F

½ cup warm water

2 tablespoons (1 ounce, 28g) unsalted butter, at room temperature

1 packet (2¼ teaspoons, 7g) instant dry yeast

1 tablespoon granulated sugar

1½ teaspoons salt

3 cups (15 ounces, 420g) all-purpose flour, divided

1 egg, beaten, for egg wash

1. Pour the warm milk and water into the bowl of a stand mixer or into a large mixing bowl. Add the butter, yeast, sugar, and salt. Mix in the stand mixer with the paddle attachment, or by hand with a wooden spoon or spatula. Add 2 cups of flour and mix until the batter looks like thick pancake batter.

2. If using a stand mixer, change to the dough hook. With the mixer running, slowly add enough of the remaining 1 cup of flour until the dough gathers on the hook and begins to pull away from the side of the bowl. Knead for 3-4 minutes to develop the dough. If mixing by hand, add the remaining flour until you can no longer stir. You might not use all of the flour. Turn the dough out onto a lightly floured surface. It should be soft and slightly sticky. Knead for about a minute to form a smooth ball. If the dough is very sticky, sprinkle with a little more flour as you knead.

3. Place the dough in an oiled bowl and flip once to coat with oil. Cover with plastic wrap or a damp kitchen towel and set aside in a warm spot to rise for 1 hour to 1 hour and 30 minutes, or until doubled in size.

4. Lightly grease a 9-by-5-inch loaf pan with vegetable oil.

5. Turn the dough out onto a floured surface and gently push it into a 12-by-8-inch rectangle. Tightly roll the dough from the short side. Set it in the prepared pan and cover with oiled plastic wrap. Set in a warm place to rise until the dough comes 1 inch over the top of the pan, 1 hour to 1 hour and 30 minutes.

6. Preheat the oven to 350°F.

7. Use a sharp knife or razor to cut a ½-inch-deep slash down the center of the loaf. Brush the top of the loaf with the egg wash.

8. Bake for 30 to 35 minutes, or until golden brown and a toothpick inserted in the center comes out clean. The interior temperature of the bread should be about 190°F. Let cool in the pan for 5 minutes before turning out onto a wire rack. Let cool to room temperature before slicing.

MAKE-AHEAD TIP: You can start making this bread the night before. Prepare the dough up to the point where it goes into the pan. Cover with plastic wrap and refrigerate overnight. In the morning, take the dough out and let it rise and bake as directed. The rise time may be a little longer since the dough will be cold.

HAMBURGER BUNS

⟩ *Makes 8 buns* ⟨

We spend lots of time thinking about what type of meat (or meat substitute) we should use to make the burger, and what type of fixings to put on top of the burger. But what about the bun? These hamburger buns are in another league from packaged buns. You'll never look back. They're soft and chewy, and have a wonderful flavor. You can start making these after lunch and have them ready for dinner—the new star of your burger. NUT-FREE

PREP TIME: 20 minutes

RISE TIME: 2 to 3 hours

BAKE TIME: 10 to 15 minutes

EQUIPMENT: Mixing bowls, electric mixer (optional), wooden spoon or spatula, baking sheet, parchment paper, pastry brush

1 cup (240 ml) whole milk, warmed to 110°F

1 packet (2¼ teaspoons, 7g) instant dry yeast

2 tablespoons (1 ounce, 28g) unsalted butter, at room temperature

2 tablespoons granulated sugar

1½ teaspoons salt

1 large egg, at room temperature, plus 1 egg white, beaten, for egg wash

3 cups (15 ounces, 435g) bread flour, divided

Sesame seeds, for garnish (optional)

1. In the bowl of a stand mixer with the paddle attachment or in a large mixing bowl, combine the milk, yeast, butter, sugar, salt, and whole egg. Mix on low speed, or by hand with a wooden spoon or spatula, to combine the ingredients. Add 2 cups of bread flour and mix until the batter is very thick.

2. If using a stand mixer, switch to the dough hook. With the mixer running, slowly add enough of the remaining 1 cup of bread flour until the dough gathers on the hook and begins to pull away from the side of the bowl. Knead 3-4 minutes to develop the dough. Turn it out onto a lightly floured surface and knead into a smooth ball. If mixing by hand, add the remaining flour until you can no longer stir (you might not use all of the flour), then turn the dough out onto a lightly floured surface to finish by hand, kneading for 2 to 3 minutes to develop the dough and form into a smooth ball.

3. Set the dough in a lightly oiled bowl, turning once to coat it with oil. Cover with plastic wrap or a damp kitchen towel and set aside to rise until doubled in volume, 1 hour to 1 hour and 30 minutes.

4. Line a baking sheet with parchment paper. Again, turn the dough out onto a lightly floured surface and knead to form a smooth ball. Divide the dough into 6 to 8 equal portions, depending on how big your burgers are. Roll each portion into a ball and set on the baking sheet. Use the palm of your hand to flatten each ball into a disk about 1 inch thick.

5. Cover the baking sheet with plastic wrap or a damp kitchen towel and allow the buns to rise until almost doubled in size, about 1 hour. Press a bun with your finger. If it springs right back, it's not ready; if the dent slowly fills in, the rolls are ready to bake.

6. Meanwhile, preheat the oven to 400°F.

7. Brush the tops of the buns with the egg white wash. Sprinkle each bun generously with sesame seeds (if desired).

8. Bake for 10 to 15 minutes, or until the buns are golden brown and feel light when lifted off the baking sheet. Let cool completely before slicing.

SUBSTITUTION TIP: Replace up to a cup of the bread flour with whole-wheat flour to make whole-wheat hamburger buns.

OVERNIGHT RYE BREAD

Makes 2 large loaves

There are two advantages to making this rye bread overnight. First of all, if you take the dough out of the refrigerator first thing in the morning, you'll have fresh bread by lunchtime. Second, that night in the refrigerator lets the dough rise very slowly. A long, slow rise enhances the flavor. This recipe makes two large loaves of bread. You can cut the recipe in half, but why? Instead, make the full recipe and freeze one of the loaves for later. DAIRY-FREE, NUT-FREE

PREP TIME: 20 minutes
RISE TIME: 2 to 3 hours, plus overnight to refrigerate
BAKE TIME: 25 to 30 minutes
EQUIPMENT: Mixing bowls, electric mixer (optional), wooden spoon or spatula, baking sheets, pastry brush

2 cups (16 ounces, 472 ml) warm water
1 tablespoon honey
1 packet (2¼ teaspoons, 7g) instant dry yeast
3 cups (15 ounces, 360g) bread flour, divided
1 cup (5.7 ounces, 160g) stone-ground rye flour
2 teaspoons salt
2 tablespoons caraway seeds, divided
1 egg white, beaten, for egg wash

1. In the bowl of a stand mixer with the paddle attachment or in large mixing bowl, combine the water, honey, yeast, 2 cups of bread flour, the rye flour, and salt. Mix on low speed, or by hand with a wooden spoon or spatula, to blend the ingredients.

2. If using a stand mixer, change to the dough hook. With the mixer running, slowly add enough of the remaining 1 cup of bread flour until the dough gathers on the hook and begins to pull away from the side of the bowl. If mixing by hand, add the remaining bread flour until you can no longer stir. You might not use all of the bread flour. Turn the dough out onto a floured surface and knead into a smooth ball. Sprinkle with flour if the dough is too wet to knead. The dough will be a little sticky.

3. Place the dough in a lightly oiled bowl, turn once to coat in oil, and cover the bowl with plastic wrap or a damp kitchen towel. Let rise for 1 hour to 1 hour and 30 minutes, or until doubled in size. Turn the dough out

onto a lightly floured surface, knead briefly, and return to the bowl. Cover tightly with plastic wrap and refrigerate overnight.

4. In the morning, remove the dough from the refrigerator and transfer to a floured surface.

5. Sprinkle the dough with 1 tablespoon of caraway seeds and knead to distribute the seeds. Knead into a smooth ball, then divide the dough in half. Shape each piece into an oblong football shape. Place the loaves on a baking sheet sprinkled liberally with cornmeal, or on a wooden peel or the back of a baking sheet if you plan to use a baking stone. Cover with oiled plastic wrap and leave in a warm place until the dough is doubled in size and springs back slowly when pressed, 1 hour to 1 hour and 30 minutes.

6. Meanwhile, preheat the oven to 400°F. If using a baking stone, place it in the oven to preheat.

7. Use a razor or sharp knife to make five diagonal slashes on top of each loaf. Brush the dough with the egg white wash and sprinkle with the remaining 1 tablespoon of caraway seeds. Slide the loaves onto the preheated stone or slide the baking sheet into the oven.

8. Bake for 25 to 30 minutes, or until the bread is nicely browned and sounds hollow when tapped. You can also use a probe thermometer to check for an internal temperature of about 200°F.

9. Let the bread cool completely before slicing.

TIME-SAVING TIP: The dough can be made and baked on the same day. Knead the dough for 3-4 minutes before the first rise and skip the step to refrigerate overnight. After the first rise, add the seeds, shape the loaves, let rise, and then bake.

PITA BREAD

≷ Makes 8 pitas ≷

If you've never baked pita at home, you'll probably be surprised how easy they are to make. It's really quite something to watch the flat rounds of dough puff up like balloons in the oven. Because this dough only needs to rise one time, it's one of the fastest bread recipes you can make. DAIRY-FREE, NUT-FREE, VEGAN

PREP TIME: 20 minutes

RISE TIME: 1 hour to 1 hour 30 minutes

BAKE TIME: 12 to 20 minutes

EQUIPMENT: Mixing bowls, electric mixer (optional), wooden spoon or spatula, baking sheet

1½ cups (12 ounces, 360 ml) warm water

1 packet (2¼ teaspoons, 7g) instant dry yeast

2 tablespoons (1 ounce, 30 ml) extra-virgin olive oil

1 tablespoon granulated sugar

1½ teaspoons salt

1 cup (5 ounces, 140g) whole-wheat flour

2½ cups (12.5 ounces, 350g) bread flour, divided

1. In the bowl of a stand mixer with the paddle attachment or in a large mixing bowl, combine the water, yeast, oil, sugar, salt, whole-wheat flour, and 1½ cups of bread flour. Mix on medium speed, or by hand with a wooden spoon or spatula, until a thick batter forms.

2. If using a stand mixer, switch to the dough hook. With the mixer running, slowly add enough of the remaining 1 cup of bread flour until the dough gathers on the hook and begins to pull away from the side of the bowl. If mixing by hand, add the remaining bread flour until you can no longer stir. You might not use all of the bread flour. Turn the dough out onto a lightly floured surface and knead into a smooth ball. The dough will be a little sticky.

3. Place the dough in a lightly oiled bowl, turn once to coat in oil, and cover the bowl with plastic wrap or a damp kitchen towel. Let rise for 1 hour to 1 hour and 30 minutes, or until doubled in size. The dough can also rise in the refrigerator overnight.

4. Preheat the oven to 450°F. If using a baking stone, place it in the oven. If you don't have a baking stone, place a baking sheet in the middle rack of the oven to preheat. If you have a dark-colored baking sheet, use that. A dark pan will absorb heat better than a light-colored pan, so the bread will bake faster.

5. Turn the dough out onto a lightly floured surface. Divide it into 8 equal pieces. Roll 2 pieces of dough out ¼ inch thick and 7 to 8 inches in diameter. Immediately place them on the preheated baking stone or baking sheet in the oven. Bake for 3 to 5 minutes, or until the pitas are puffed and the bottoms are deeply browned. You don't need to flip the bread. Remove the baked breads and wrap in a clean kitchen towel while you continue rolling and baking the remaining pitas (in three more batches).

6. Though best used the day they are made, these pitas also freeze very well.

BAKING TIP: To make white pita bread, use 1 cup all-purpose flour in place of the whole-wheat flour. You can bake pitas on the stove top on a griddle or frying pan; simply bake on the first side for 1 to 2 minutes, flip, and bake on the other side until the bread puffs up.

DUTCH TIGER BREAD

≥ Makes 8 rolls ≤

This is a recipe unlike any other. A soft, slightly sweet bread is coated with topping made with rice flour and yeast. As the bread rises and bakes, that topping becomes super crunchy and crackles on the surface of the bread. In fact, this is one of the crunchiest breads you'll ever taste. NUT-FREE

PREP TIME: 30 minutes

RISE TIME: 1 hour 30 minutes

BAKE TIME: 20 to 25 minutes

EQUIPMENT: Mixing bowls, electric mixer (optional), wooden spoon or spatula, baking sheet, parchment paper or silicone baking mat, whisk, pastry brush

FOR THE DOUGH

½ cup (4 ounces, 120 ml) warm water

1 cup (8 ounces, 240 ml) warm whole milk

1 tablespoon unsalted butter (.5 ounce, 15g), melted

1 tablespoon granulated sugar

1 packet (2¼ teaspoons, 7g) instant dry yeast

1½ teaspoons salt

½ cup (2.5 ounces, 75g) whole-wheat flour

3 cups (15 ounces, 420g) all-purpose flour, divided

FOR THE TOPPING

1 cup (6 ounces, 170g) rice flour

1 packet (2¼ teaspoons, 7g) instant dry yeast

1 tablespoon granulated sugar

½ teaspoon salt

1 tablespoon vegetable oil

¾ cup (6 oz, 180ml) warm water

TO MAKE THE DOUGH

1. In the bowl of a stand mixer with the paddle attachment, or in a large mixing bowl using a wooden spoon or spatula, mix the water, milk, butter, sugar, yeast, and salt. Add the whole-wheat flour and 2 cups of all-purpose flour. Mix until a thick batter forms.

2. If using a stand mixer, switch to the dough hook. With the mixer running, slowly add enough of the remaining ½ cup of all-purpose flour until the dough gathers on the hook and begins to pull away from the side of the bowl. Knead 3-4 minutes to develop the dough. If mixing by hand, add the remaining all-purpose flour until you can no longer stir. You may not use all of the all-purpose flour. Turn the dough out onto a floured surface and knead into a smooth ball.

3. Transfer the dough to a lightly oiled bowl, turning once to coat. Cover the bowl with plastic wrap or a damp kitchen towel and set aside to rise until doubled in volume, about 1 hour. Line a baking sheet with parchment paper or a silicone baking mat.

4. Turn the dough out onto a lightly floured surface and divide into 8 equal portions. Roll each piece of dough into a smooth ball and set on the prepared baking sheet. Cover the rolls with a damp kitchen towel and preheat the oven to 400°F while you mix the topping.

TO MAKE THE TOPPING

1. Whisk together the rice flour, yeast, sugar, and salt. Add the oil to the warm water, then pour into the dry ingredients, whisking until combined. Set the topping aside for 20 minutes, until bubbly.

2. Uncover the rolls and brush generously with the topping. Let the rolls rise for another 20 minutes.

3. Bake for 20 to 25 minutes, or until golden brown. Transfer to a wire rack and let cool to room temperature.

TECHNIQUE TIP: This dough can be formed into one large loaf instead of eight individual rolls.

SOFT PRETZELS

⋛ Makes 12 pretzels ⋚

These pretzels are a wonderful, homey snack. If you have kids in the house, you know they'll enjoy forming the pretzel shape, and then making them disappear. These pretzels are delicious with a squiggle of mustard or dipped into cheese sauce. DAIRY-FREE, NUT-FREE

PREP TIME: 20 minutes
RISE TIME: 1 hour to 1 hour 30 minutes
BAKE TIME: 15 to 20 minutes
EQUIPMENT: Mixing bowls, electric mixer (optional), wooden spoon or spatula, baking sheets, parchment paper or silicone baking mats, pastry brush

1½ cups (12 ounces, 360 ml) warm water
1 tablespoon granulated sugar
1 packet (2¼ teaspoons, 7g) instant dry yeast
1½ teaspoons table salt
3 cups (15 ounces, 425g) all-purpose flour, divided
2 quarts (about 2 liters) water
⅓ cup (2.5 ounces, 70g) baking soda
1 egg white, beaten, for egg wash (omit for vegan recipe)
Coarse salt, for sprinkling
Seeds such as poppy, sesame, and caraway, for garnish (optional)

1. In the bowl of a stand mixer with the paddle attachment or in a large mixing bowl using a wooden spoon or spatula, mix the warm water, sugar, yeast, and table salt. With the mixer running on low, add 2 cups of flour and mix to form a smooth batter, or mix in the flour by hand.

2. If using a stand mixer, switch to the dough hook. With the mixer running, slowly add enough of the remaining 1 cup of flour until the dough gathers on the hook and begins to pull away from the side of the bowl. Knead 3-4 minutes to develop the dough. If mixing with a wooden spoon or spatula, add the remaining flour until you can no longer stir, then finish kneading in the flour by hand. You may not use all of the flour.

3. Turn the dough out onto a lightly floured surface and knead into a smooth ball. Place it in an oiled bowl, turning once to coat, then cover with plastic wrap or a damp kitchen towel and set aside to rise until doubled in volume, 1 thour to 1 hour and 30 minutes.

4. Preheat the oven to 475°F. Line two baking sheets with parchment paper or silicone baking mats and brush with vegetable oil.

5. In a large pot, bring 2 quarts of water and the baking soda to a boil while shaping the pretzels.

6. Turn the dough out onto a floured surface and divide it into 12 equal pieces. Shape each piece into a 20- to 24-inch-long rope. The longer and thinner the rope, the more open the pretzel shape will be.

7. To form a pretzel, lift the dough rope on either end and allow the middle to sit on the floured surface, forming a U shape. Twist the ends of the rope together two times, then fold the twist over and rest it on the center of the U. Lift the pretzel by the two top loops and place on oiled parchment paper. Repeat to shape the rest of the pretzels.

8. Once the baking soda water is boiling, drop 2 to 3 pretzels at a time into the water for 30 seconds. Transfer the boiled pretzels to a wire rack and let them drain while you boil the remaining pretzels.

9. Transfer the pretzels to the prepared baking sheets. Brush each pretzel with egg white wash and sprinkle with coarse salt and the seeds of your choice (if desired). Bake for 15 to 20 minutes, or until puffed and golden brown.

10. The pretzels are best served warm. Leftover pretzels can be frozen for up to 3 months. Let thaw, then warm briefly in a 350°F oven before serving.

SHORTCUT TIP: Boiling the unbaked pretzels in baking soda water gives them their characteristic color and flavor. You can skip the boiling step and instead brush the hot pretzels with melted butter for a pretzel like you get at the mall.

BUTTERMILK DINNER ROLLS

Makes 16 to 24 rolls

These dinner rolls are perfectly soft and slightly sweet, with a beautiful golden-brown crust. The buttermilk in the dough adds richness and a tangy flavor. Present them at your next holiday dinner for a welcome response. NUT-FREE

PREP TIME: 20 minutes

RISE TIME: 2 hours

BAKE TIME: 10 to 15 minutes

EQUIPMENT: Mixing bowls, electric mixer (optional), wooden spoon or spatula, baking sheet, parchment paper or silicone baking mat, pastry brush

2 cups (16 ounces, 500 ml) buttermilk, at room temperature

1 tablespoon granulated sugar

1 packet (2¼ teaspoons, 7g) instant dry yeast

1 egg, at room temperature

1½ teaspoons salt

1 stick (4 ounces, 115g) butter, melted, divided

4½ cups (22.5 ounces, 630g) bread flour, divided

1. In the bowl of a stand mixer with the paddle attachment or a large mixing bowl, add the buttermilk, sugar, yeast, egg, salt, and ¼ cup of melted butter. Mix on low speed, or by hand with a wooden spoon or spatula, to combine the ingredients. Add 2½ cups of flour and mix to combine.

2. If you're using a stand mixer, switch to the dough hook. With the mixer running, slowly add enough of the remaining 2 cups of flour until the dough gathers on the hook and begins to pull away from the side of the bowl. You may not use all of the flour. Knead on medium for 3 minutes, then reduce the speed to low. If mixing by hand, knead the remaining flour in by hand, then continue kneading for 5 minutes. Turn the dough out onto a lightly floured surface and knead into a smooth ball. The dough should be soft and smooth.

3. Place the dough in an oiled bowl, turning once to coat, then cover with plastic wrap or a damp kitchen towel and set in a warm place until doubled in size, 1 hour and 30 minutes to 2 hours.

4. Turn the dough out onto a lightly floured surface and cut it into 16 to 24 even pieces, depending on how large you want the rolls to be. (They'll bake up at least twice the size of the dough ball.) Roll each piece of dough to form a smooth ball.

5. Place the rolls on a baking sheet lined with parchment paper or a silicone baking mat. Brush the tops with some of the remaining melted butter. Set aside in a warm spot to rise until nearly doubled in size and the dough springs back slowly when poked, about 1 hour.

6. Preheat the oven to 375°F.

7. Bake the rolls for 10 to 15 minutes, or until golden brown. As soon as the rolls come out of the oven, brush the tops with more melted butter. Serve warm or at room temperature.

MAKE-AHEAD TIP: You can prepare the recipe through step 4 and then freeze the dough balls. Before proceeding with the rest of the recipe, let the dough balls thaw. The baked rolls can also be frozen and warmed in a 200°F oven before serving.

CINNAMON-SUGAR DOUGHNUTS

Makes 8 to 12 doughnuts

Generally, there are two kinds of doughnuts. Cakey doughnuts are made from a biscuit type of dough, and yeast doughnuts are made with bread dough. I always prefer yeast-style. These doughnuts are made from my enriched bread dough. This same dough can be used to make Cinnamon Rolls (page 192) or Monkey Bread (page 190). Learn one recipe and make three different treats. NUT-FREE

PREP TIME: 35 minutes

RISE TIME: 2 to 2 hours 30 minutes

COOK TIME: 15 to 25 minutes

EQUIPMENT: Mixing bowls, electric mixer (optional), wooden spoon or spatula, baking sheets, parchment paper or silicone baking mats, lidded oven-safe pot

1 cup (8 ounces, 240 ml) warm milk, at 110°F

1 cup (8 ounces, 224g) granulated sugar, divided

4 tablespoons (2 ounces, 60g) unsalted butter, melted

1 egg, at room temperature

1 packet (2¼ teaspoons, 7g) instant dry yeast

3½ cups (17.5 ounces, 490g) all-purpose flour, divided

1 teaspoon salt

Vegetable oil, for frying

2 teaspoons ground cinnamon

1. In the bowl of a stand mixer with the paddle attachment or a large mixing bowl, combine the warm milk, ¼ cup of sugar, the melted butter, egg, and yeast. Add 2 cups of flour and the salt. Mix on medium speed, or by hand using a wooden spoon or spatula, for 2 minutes.

2. If you're using a stand mixer, switch to the dough hook. With the mixer on low speed, add the remaining 1½ cups of flour, ½ cup at a time. The dough should be soft and elastic and will gather on the hook and begin to pull away from the side of the bowl. Knead for 2 to 3 minutes. If mixing by hand, knead in the remaining flour by hand, then continue to knead for 5 minutes. Turn the dough out onto a lightly floured surface and knead into a smooth ball. Place the dough in a lightly oiled bowl, turning once to coat. Cover with plastic wrap or a damp kitchen towel and leave at room temperature to rise until doubled in volume, about 1 hour and 30 minutes.

3. On a lightly floured surface, roll the dough out ½ inch thick. Use a 3- to 4-inch round cutter to cut doughnuts. Use a smaller cutter to cut out a center hole. Place the doughnuts 2 inches apart on two baking sheets lined with parchment paper. Re-roll the scraps of dough and continue cutting doughnuts until all the dough is used up.

4. Cover the doughnuts with plastic wrap and set aside to rise until the dough springs back slowly when poked, 30 minutes to 1 hour. If the dough bounces right back, the doughnuts are not quite ready to bake. The time this takes will vary based on the temperature of the room.

5. Meanwhile, in a large Dutch oven or other heavy pot, heat 2 inches of oil to 350°F. Combine the remaining ¾ cup of sugar with the cinnamon in a shallow bowl or pie plate.

6. Fry the doughnuts a couple at a time, 2 to 3 minutes per side, or until golden brown and puffy. As you take each doughnut out of the oil, immediately roll it in the cinnamon sugar to coat completely.

7. Transfer each cinnamon-sugar doughnut to a wire rack to cool while you fry the rest. Enjoy warm or within a couple of hours of frying.

MAKE-AHEAD TIP: If you want fresh doughnuts for breakfast, you can make this dough the day before. Place the covered dough in the refrigerator overnight. Roll, cut, and fry the doughnuts in the morning.

MONKEY BREAD

⇒ *Serves 12* ⇐

Monkey bread is as fun to eat as the name suggests. Set this big, beautiful loaf on the table and allow your guests to tear off individual chunks of gooey bread. Monkey bread is made from my enriched bread dough. This same dough can be used to make Cinnamon Rolls (page 192) or Cinnamon-Sugar Doughnuts (page 188). NUT-FREE

PREP TIME: 30 minutes
RISE TIME: 2 hours 30 minutes
BAKE TIME: 25 to 30 minutes
EQUIPMENT: Mixing bowls, electric mixer (optional), wooden spoon or spatula, 12-cup Bundt pan

FOR THE DOUGH

1½ cups (12 ounces, 360 ml) warm milk, at 110°F
⅓ cup (3 ounces, 84g) granulated sugar
6 tablespoons (3 ounces, 84g) unsalted butter, melted
2 eggs, at room temperature
1 packet (2¼ teaspoons, 7g) instant dry yeast
5 cups (25 ounces, 700g) all-purpose flour, divided
1½ teaspoons salt
1 teaspoon ground cinnamon
½ teaspoon ground cardamom (optional)

FOR THE COATING

1 cup (8 ounces, 224g) packed brown sugar
1 tablespoon ground cinnamon
1 stick (4 ounces, 112g) unsalted butter, melted
⅓ teaspoon salt
1 cup (4 ounces, 112g) confectioners' sugar
1 tablespoon plus 2 teaspoons whole milk
½ teaspoon vanilla extract

TO MAKE THE DOUGH

1. In the bowl of a stand mixer with the paddle attachment or a large mixing bowl, combine the warm milk, granulated sugar, melted butter, eggs, and yeast. Add 3 cups of flour, the salt, cinnamon, and cardamom (if using). Mix on medium speed, or by hand with a wooden spoon or spatula, for 2 minutes.

2. If using a stand mixer, change to the dough hook. With the mixer on low speed, add the remaining 2 cups of flour, ½ cup at a time. The dough should be soft and elastic and will gather on the hook and begin to pull away from the side of the bowl. Knead for 2 to 3 minutes. If mixing by hand, knead in the remaining flour by hand, then continue kneading for 5 minutes.

3. Turn the dough out onto a lightly floured surface and knead into a smooth ball. Place the dough in a lightly oiled bowl, turning once to coat. Cover with plastic wrap or a damp kitchen towel and leave at room temperature to rise until doubled in volume, about 1 hour and 30 minutes.

TO MAKE THE COATING AND ASSEMBLE THE BREAD

1. Generously butter a 12-cup Bundt pan. In a small bowl, stir together the brown sugar and cinnamon. In another bowl, stir together the melted butter and salt.

2. Turn the dough out onto a lightly floured surface and knead briefly. Divide the dough into 48 pieces. Roll each piece into a ball, dip the ball into the melted butter, then roll it in the brown sugar–cinnamon mix. Place the coated dough balls into the prepared pan. Pour any remaining melted butter and cinnamon sugar over the top of the bread. Cover the pan and set it aside in a warm place until the dough comes almost to the top of the pan, about 1 hour, or set the pan in the refrigerator overnight.

3. Preheat the oven to 350°F.

4. Bake the bread for 30 minutes, or until puffy and golden brown. While the bread bakes, stir together the confectioners' sugar, milk, and vanilla.

5. Let the bread cool in the pan for 5 minutes, then flip it onto a serving platter. Drizzle the glaze all over the bread or serve as a dipping sauce. Enjoy warm from the oven.

VARIATION TIP: Cream Cheese Frosting (page 102) is also a wonderful dip for monkey bread.

CINNAMON ROLLS

Makes 12 rolls

Does anything in the world smell as good as freshly baked cinnamon rolls? Top these warm buns with Cream Cheese Frosting (page 102) for an extra special treat. These cinnamon rolls are made from my enriched bread dough. This same dough can be used to make Monkey Bread (page 190) or Cinnamon-Sugar Doughnuts (page 188). NUT-FREE

PREP TIME: 30 minutes

RISE TIME: 2 hours 30 minutes, plus overnight to refrigerate (optional)

BAKE TIME: 25 to 30 minutes

EQUIPMENT: Mixing bowls, electric mixer, wooden spoon or spatula, 9-by-13-inch baking pan, rolling pin, pastry brush

1 cup (8 ounces, 240 ml) warm milk, at 110°F

¼ cup (2 ounces, 56g) granulated sugar, plus ⅓ cup (3 ounces, 84g)

1½ sticks (6 ounces, 168g) unsalted butter, melted, divided

1 egg

1 packet (2¼ teaspoons, 7g) instant dry yeast

3½ cups (17.5 ounces, 490g) all-purpose flour, divided

1 teaspoon salt

⅓ cup (3 ounces, 84g) packed brown sugar

1 tablespoon ground cinnamon

4 tablespoons (2 ounces, 56g) softened unsalted butter, at room temperature

¾ cup (3 ounces, 84g) confectioners' sugar

¼ cup (2 ounces, 56g) cream cheese, at room temperature

½ teaspoon vanilla extract

1. In the bowl of a stand mixer with the paddle attachment or a large mixing bowl, combine the warm milk, ¼ cup of granulated sugar, ¼ cup of melted butter, the egg, and yeast. Add 2 cups of flour and the salt. Mix on medium speed, or by hand using a wooden spoon or spatula, for 2 minutes.

2. If using a stand mixer, change to the dough hook. With the mixer on low, add the remaining 1½ cups of flour, ½ cup at a time. The dough should be soft and elastic and will gather on the hook and begin to pull away from the side of the bowl. Knead for 2 to 3 minutes. If mixing by hand, knead in the flour by hand, then continue kneading for 5 minutes.

3. Turn the dough out onto a lightly floured surface and knead into a smooth ball. Place the dough in a lightly oiled bowl, turning once to coat. Cover with plastic wrap or a damp kitchen towel and leave at room temperature to rise until doubled in volume, about 1 hour and 30 minutes.

4. Liberally butter a 9-by-13-inch baking pan. In a small bowl, combine the remaining ⅓ cup of granulated sugar, the brown sugar, and cinnamon. Turn the dough out onto a lightly floured surface. Roll to a 12-by-16-inch rectangle. Reserve 2 tablespoons of the remaining melted butter, then brush the surface of the dough with the remaining melted butter. Sprinkle with the cinnamon sugar.

5. Working from the long side of the dough rectangle, tightly roll the dough into a log, pinching the seam to seal. Use a serrated knife to cut the log into 12 rolls. Place the rolls in the prepared pan. Brush the tops with the reserved 2 tablespoons of melted butter. If baking the same day, allow the rolls to rise for about 1 hour, or until puffy and almost filling the pan. If baking the next day, cover with plastic wrap and refrigerate overnight. In the morning, remove the rolls from the refrigerator and let rise.

6. Preheat the oven to 375°F.

7. Bake the cinnamon rolls for 25 to 30 minutes, or until golden brown.

8. While the rolls are baking, make the icing. In a large mixing bowl, using an electric mixer, cream the softened butter and confectioners' sugar until well combined. Add the cream cheese and whip until well aerated. Mix in the vanilla.

9. While the cinnamon rolls are still warm, transfer them from the pan to a serving plate. Spread the icing generously over the rolls and serve immediately.

MAKE-AHEAD TIP: After filling and rolling the dough into a log, wrap tightly in two layers of plastic wrap. Freeze for up to 3 months. Let the dough thaw overnight in the refrigerator, then proceed with the recipe as directed.

FRESH BERRY BREAKFAST FOCACCIA

≥ Serves 12 ≤

This focaccia made with fresh berries is a nice change from the typically sweet and rich breakfast pastries. This super light and airy bread is simply topped with fresh berries, some optional sliced almonds, and just as much sugar as you'd like. This is lovely with a cup of coffee and maybe a little yogurt on the side.

PREP TIME: 30 minutes

RISE TIME: 2 hours 30 minutes to 3 hours, plus overnight to refrigerate

BAKE TIME: 25 to 30 minutes

EQUIPMENT: Mixing bowls, electric mixer (optional), wooden spoon or spatula, baking sheet, pastry brush

1¾ cups (14 ounces, 420 ml) warm water

1 packet (2¼ teaspoons, 7g) instant dry yeast

¼ cup (1.75 ounces, 52.5 ml) extra-virgin olive oil

1½ teaspoons salt

4¼ cups (22 ounces, 616g) all-purpose flour, divided

1 egg, beaten, for egg wash

Demerara or granulated sugar, for sprinkling

2 pints fresh blueberries, raspberries, and/or blackberries

½ cup sliced almonds (optional)

1. In the bowl of a stand mixer with the paddle attachment or a large mixing bowl, combine the water, yeast, oil, and salt. Add 2 cups of flour and mix on medium speed to combine (use a wooden spoon or spatula if mixing by hand). Cover with plastic wrap and let the batter rest for 20 minutes.

2. If using a stand mixer, switch to the dough hook and add the remaining 2¼ cups of flour. Knead on medium-low speed for 20 minutes. The dough will be quite sticky but should also be very stretchy. If working by hand, you may want to use a plastic bowl scraper to help you knead the wet dough. Scrape the dough into a lightly oiled bowl, turning once to coat. Cover with plastic wrap or a damp kitchen towel and set aside in a warm place until doubled in volume, 1 hour and 30 minutes to 2 hours.

3. Knead the dough, return it to the bowl, cover, and refrigerate overnight.

4. In the morning, take the dough out of the refrigerator. Preheat the oven to 400°F. Lightly oil a baking sheet with olive oil. Carefully place the cold dough on the oiled baking sheet and flip it over to coat with a film of oil. Use your fingers to spread the dough about ½ inch thick.

5. Allow the dough to rise for about 1 hour, until a finger poked in the dough leaves a dimple. Lightly brush the top of the dough with egg wash and sprinkle lightly with sugar. Use your fingers to dimple the top of the dough all over. Press the berries into the dough, spacing them evenly over the focaccia. Add the almonds (if desired).

6. Bake for 25 to 30 minutes, or until puffed and golden brown. Enjoy the focaccia warm or at room temperature.

TECHNIQUE TIP: Focaccia is all about the gluten and a wet dough. Long kneading is necessary for a good texture.

MULTIGRAIN ENGLISH MUFFINS

> *Makes 16 muffins*

These multigrain English muffins are surprisingly easy to make and so much better than store-bought versions. Spend 30 minutes of hands-on time and stock up your freezer for future breakfasts. NUT-FREE

PREP TIME: 30 minutes
RISE TIME: 1 hour 45 minutes to 2 hours 30 minutes
COOK TIME: 30 to 45 minutes
EQUIPMENT: Mixing bowls, electric mixer (optional), wooden spoon or spatula, biscuit cutter (optional), baking sheet, griddle or frying pan

1 cup (8 ounces, 240 ml) very
    warm water
1 cup (8 ounces, 240 ml) whole milk,
    warmed to 110°F
1 packet (2¼ teaspoons, 7g) instant
    dry yeast
¼ cup (2.5 ounces, 75g) honey
¼ cup (1.75 ounces, 52.5 ml) vegetable oil
½ cup (2.5 ounces, 70g)
    whole-wheat flour
½ cup (2 ounces, 56g) wheat germ
½ cup (1.75 ounces, 45g) rolled oats
2 teaspoons salt
4 cups (20 ounces, 560g) all-purpose
    flour, divided
Cornmeal, for sprinkling the
    work surface

1. In the bowl of a stand mixer with the paddle attachment or a large mixing bowl, combine the water, milk, yeast, honey, oil, whole-wheat flour, wheat germ, oats, salt, and 2 cups of all-purpose flour. Mix on low speed, or by hand with a wooden spoon or spatula, until blended.

2. If using a stand mixer, switch to the dough hook. Add the remaining 2 cups of all-purpose flour, ½ cup at a time, until the dough gathers on the hook and begins to pull away from the side of the bowl. Knead the dough for 2 to 3 minutes. If mixing by hand, add the remaining all-purpose flour until you can no longer stir, then turn the dough out onto a floured surface to finish kneading by hand for 6 to 7 minutes. You may not use all of the all-purpose flour.

3. Place the dough in an oiled bowl, turning once to coat. Cover with plastic wrap or a damp kitchen towel and let rise in a warm place until doubled in volume, 1 hour to 1 hour and 30 minutes.

4. While the dough is still in the bowl, punch it down to deflate. Lightly sprinkle a work surface with cornmeal. Turn the dough out onto the work surface and roll the dough out ½ inch thick. Use a 3-inch biscuit cutter or the rim of a glass to cut out muffins. Re-roll the scraps and continue cutting until all the dough is used. You should get about 16 muffins. Place the muffins on an ungreased baking sheet. Cover and let rise until doubled in volume, 45 minutes to 1 hour.

5. Preheat a griddle or frying pan over medium-high heat. Lightly oil the pan, then, working in batches, cook the muffins for about 8 minutes on each side, or until well risen and deep golden brown. Let cool on a wire rack. Split and toast before serving.

STORAGE TIP: These English muffins freeze very well.

ROSEMARY & OLIVE FOCACCIA *page 209*

Chapter 8

SAVORY BAKED GOODS

QUICK TUTORIAL

About Savory Baked Goods

When we think about baking, most of us probably immediately think of sweets and desserts. Why wouldn't we, since most baked goods do tend toward the sweet side of things? However, you may be surprised to realize how many of the recipes and techniques that are covered in this book can be adapted to create savory dishes.

For example, did you know that zucchini is, botanically, a fruit? With that in mind, it's easy to imagine that zucchini can be baked into a pie like any other fruit. Layer the zucchini with ricotta cheese and a few other savory ingredients, and you've got a delicious, nutritious, and savory pie recipe.

It's really just a short leap from a shortbread cookie to an Oatmeal Crispbread (page 203). You'll find that the knowledge you learn in the cookie chapter can be applied to making healthy and savory snacks as well.

Helpful Hints

◆ The more you bake, the more you'll see that some of the recipes in this chapter can be mixed and matched to create new dishes. If you have a little beef stew left over from making Beef & Guinness Potpie (page 220), you can fold that filling into the dough for Empanadas (page 222) or Samosas (page 217) to make a savory hand pie.

◆ The filling from the Roasted Veggie Pasties (page 215) can be baked in a pie shell, or you can encase the filling in flaky pastry to create a savory galette. You might adapt the Margherita Pizza recipe (page 211) to make homemade calzones. This just requires you to layer the filling on half of the dough, then fold the dough over the filling and bake until golden brown.

Shortcuts/Time-Savers

◆ While this book promotes mostly "from scratch" recipes, who's to judge? If you don't have time to make your own, you can use frozen pizza dough in recipes, and it will still be delicious.

◆ Planning ahead will also help you create dishes on a dime. For example, frozen Quick Puff Pastry (page 144) can be used for both Beef & Guinness Potpie (page 220) and Cheese Straws (page 205). You can use premade pie dough to make Zucchini & Ricotta Pie (page 213) or Roasted Veggie Pasties (page 215).

◆ To help along your Empanadas (page 222), many large groceries carry premade empanada wrappers in the Latin section. And for a quick round of Samosas (page 217), use rounds of puff pastry, phyllo dough, or wonton wrappers.

FLAKY BUTTERMILK BISCUITS

Makes 12 biscuits

I worked for a long time trying to create a recipe for buttermilk biscuits that are both fluffy and flaky. It's all about how you handle the dough. This dough should be made by hand to yield very tender biscuits. NUT-FREE

PREP TIME: 20 minutes

BAKE TIME: 10 to 12 minutes

EQUIPMENT: Baking sheet, parchment paper or silicone baking mat, mixing bowls, whisk, biscuit cutter (optional)

2 cups (10 ounces, 280g) all-purpose flour

2 cups (8.5 ounces, 240g) cake flour

1 tablespoon plus 1 teaspoon baking powder

1 teaspoon baking soda

2 teaspoons granulated sugar

1 teaspoon salt

2 sticks (8 ounces, 225g) cold unsalted butter, cut into 16 pieces

2 cups (16 ounces, 450g) buttermilk, plus more for brushing

BAKING TIP: If the bottoms of the biscuits are browning too fast, set another baking pan under the biscuits after 5 minutes of baking, or move them up a rack in the oven. Baked biscuits can be frozen for several weeks. Thaw, then warm in a 200°F oven.

1. Preheat the oven to 400°F. Line a baking sheet with parchment paper or a silicone baking mat.

2. In a large mixing bowl, combine the all-purpose flour, cake flour, baking powder, baking soda, sugar, and salt. Whisk the dry ingredients to combine. Mix the butter into the flour with your fingers until it's broken down into bits slightly larger than pea-size. Add the 2 cups of buttermilk all at once and mix until about two-thirds of the dry ingredients are absorbed.

3. Turn the dough out onto a lightly floured surface and gently knead together 6 to 8 times, just to incorporate the remaining dry flour. Gently pat the dough ½ inch thick, brush off the excess flour, and fold the dough in half, then fold again. Pat the dough ¾ inch thick. Use a 3-inch biscuit cutter or the rim of a glass to cut as many biscuits as you can. Gather the scraps together and continue cutting to use up all the dough.

4. Set the biscuits on the prepared baking sheet and brush the tops with buttermilk.

5. Bake for 10 to 12 minutes, until golden brown. The biscuits are best eaten warm from the oven.

PEANUT BUTTER DOG BISCUITS

Makes 18 biscuits

Even though no one really *needs* to make dog biscuits at home, this is a fun project, especially if you have kids in the house. The dough comes together very quickly, is endlessly adaptable, and is chock-full of healthy ingredients for your canine best friend.

PREP TIME: 10 minutes

BAKE TIME: 15 to 20 minutes

EQUIPMENT: Baking sheet, parchment paper or silicone baking mat, mixing bowl, rolling pin, cookie cutters

½ cup (5 ounces, 140g) applesauce
⅓ cup (3.5 ounces, 98g) peanut butter
1 egg
½ teaspoon salt
1 teaspoon baking powder
1 cup (3 ounces, 85g) old-fashioned rolled oats
1 to 1½ cups (5 to 7.5 ounces, 140g to 210g) whole-wheat flour

CANINE CAUTION: You can adapt these ingredients, but make sure whatever ingredient you add is okay for dogs to eat. Don't use chocolate, onions, garlic, raisins, or grapes, which are all dangerous for them to eat.

1. Preheat the oven to 350°F. Line a baking sheet with parchment paper.

2. In a large mixing bowl, combine the applesauce and peanut butter until smooth. Add the egg and mix to combine.

3. Add the salt, baking powder, and oats. For softer biscuits, add 1 cup of flour. For crunchier biscuits, add 1½ cups of flour.

4. Turn the dough out onto a lightly floured surface. Knead the dough into a smooth ball, adding a little more flour if it is very sticky.

5. Roll the dough ¼ inch thick. Using cookie cutters, cut out desired shapes and put on the prepared baking sheet. Using a 3½-inch bone-shaped cutter, you'll get about 18 biscuits. If you want extra-crispy biscuits, roll the dough ⅛ inch thick.

6. Bake for 15 to 20 minutes, or until crisp and lightly golden brown. Let cool completely, if your dog will let you wait that long.

OATMEAL CRISPBREAD

Makes 32 crackers

This crispbread is a healthy, cracker-like bread that is perfect for lunch or snack time. The dough comes together like a biscuit dough and is rolled very thin for a crisp finish. The baked crackers keep for days in an airtight container. NUT-FREE

PREP TIME: 20 minutes

BAKE TIME: 15 to 20

EQUIPMENT: Mixing bowls, whisk, electric mixer, rolling pin, baking sheets, parchment paper or silicone baking mats

1 cup (3.5 ounces, 100g) rolled oats, plus ¼ cup (2 ounces, 60g), roughly chopped, for topping

¾ cup (3.75 ounces, 105g) all-purpose flour

¾ cup (3.75 ounces, 105g) stone-ground whole-wheat flour

1 teaspoon salt

½ teaspoon baking soda

6 tablespoons (3 ounces, 84g) unsalted butter, at room temperature

1 tablespoon granulated sugar

1 tablespoon honey

¾ cup (6 ounces, 180 ml) buttermilk

1. Preheat the oven to 350°F.

2. In a large bowl, whisk together 1 cup of rolled oats, the all-purpose flour, whole-wheat flour, salt, and baking soda. Set aside.

3. In another large bowl, using an electric mixer, cream together the butter, sugar, and honey until light and fluffy. Alternate adding the dry ingredients and the buttermilk, and mix just until combined. The dough should be soft and slightly sticky.

4. Turn the dough out onto a lightly floured surface and divide it in half. Roll one piece of dough into a rectangle about ¼ inch thick, sprinkling with enough flour to keep it from sticking to the surface.

Continued

5. Transfer the dough to a 16-by-12-inch sheet of parchment paper and continue rolling until it is less than ⅛ inch thick and the size of the paper. Trim the edges to make a neat rectangle. Sprinkle the remaining ¼ cup of chopped oats over the surface and press them into the dough. Prick the dough all over with a fork and score the dough into 16 rectangles or to your desired cracker size. Repeat with the second piece of dough and another piece of parchment paper.

6. Transfer the dough, still on the parchment paper, to two baking sheets. Bake for 15 to 20 minutes, until golden brown and crisp.

7. Let the crackers cool on a rack for 5 minutes before breaking along scores. They can be stored in a sealed container for up to a week.

TECHNIQUE TIP: I find it easiest to finish rolling the dough right on the parchment paper to get it as thin as possible. If you don't have parchment paper, you can lightly butter the back of a baking sheet, then transfer the partially rolled dough to it. Finish rolling until it almost covers the back of the baking sheet. Continue with the recipe as directed. Also, once the crackers are baked, it's easier to break them while they're still slightly warm.

CHEESE STRAWS

Makes 24 straws

If you need a quick and easy appetizer recipe, make these cheese straws for something fun and different. They take just a few minutes to put together and can be served warm or at room temperature. NUT-FREE

PREP TIME: 20 minutes, plus 15 to 30 minutes to chill

BAKE TIME: 10 to 15 minutes

EQUIPMENT: Baking sheets, parchment paper or silicone baking mats, rolling pin, pastry brush, pizza cutter (optional)

½ recipe Quick Puff Pastry (page 144) or 2 sheets frozen puff pastry

1 egg, beaten, for egg wash

1 teaspoon paprika

⅛ teaspoon cayenne pepper (optional)

¾ cup (2.25 ounces, 63g) freshly grated Parmesan cheese

1. Line two baking sheets with parchment paper or silicone baking mats.

2. Place the pastry dough on a lightly floured surface. Roll to a 12-by-16-inch rectangle, about ⅛ inch thick. Turn the rectangle so the 12-inch side is facing you.

3. Brush the dough with egg wash. Mix the paprika and cayenne pepper (if using) with the grated cheese. Sprinkle the cheese over the bottom half of the dough. Fold the top half of the dough over the filling to form an 8-by-12-inch rectangle.

4. Use a rolling pin to lightly roll over the dough to adhere the two sides. Use a pizza cutter or sharp knife to cut the dough into ½-inch strips. You'll get 24 strips.

Continued

5. Take a strip of dough and twist the ends in opposite directions to form a spiral. Gently stretch and twist the strip to form a 12-inch-long straw. Place the straw on a prepared baking sheet, pressing either end into place to help keep the spiral from unraveling. Repeat with the remaining strips, fitting 12 on each baking sheet.

6. Transfer the baking sheets to the refrigerator and let chill for 15 to 30 minutes. Meanwhile, preheat the oven to 425°F.

7. Bake the cheese straws for 10 to 15 minutes, or until golden brown. Serve slightly warm or at room temperature.

MAKE-AHEAD TIP: The assembled straws can be frozen for up to a month before baking. Freeze on a tray so the straws don't break.

PUMPKIN-SAGE PULL-APART BREAD

Serves 8

Pumpkin and sage are a wonderful flavor combination. This bread can be made at any time of year, but it would certainly be at home on the Thanksgiving table. Pull-apart breads are a lot of fun to serve. You don't need to slice the bread. As the name suggests, your guests simply pull off a slice and enjoy. NUT-FREE

PREP TIME: 30 minutes, plus 2 hours to rise

BAKE TIME: 40 to 45 minutes

EQUIPMENT: Microwave-safe bowl, mixing bowls, electric mixer (optional), 9-by-5-inch loaf pan, parchment paper, pastry brush, food processor (optional), rolling pin, pizza cutter (optional)

FOR THE DOUGH

¼ cup (2 ounces, 60 ml) warm water

¾ cup (6 ounces, 168g) canned pumpkin purée, at room temperature

¾ cup (6 ounces, 168g) full-fat Greek yogurt, at room temperature

1 packet (2¼ teaspoons, 7g) instant dry yeast

2 tablespoons honey

1 large egg, at room temperature

1 teaspoon salt

3½ cups (17.5 ounces, 490g) all-purpose flour, divided

Olive oil, for brushing

FOR THE FILLING

2 large garlic cloves

½ cup (2 large sprigs) fresh sage leaves

½ cup (1.5 ounces, 42g) grated Parmesan cheese

¼ cup (1.75 ounces, 52.5 ml) extra-virgin olive oil

TO MAKE THE DOUGH

1. In a microwave-safe bowl, combine the water, pumpkin, and yogurt. Warm in the microwave in 30-second increments until the mixture is 110°F to 120°F, or slightly warmer than body temperature.

2. Transfer the mixture to the bowl of a stand mixer or a large mixing bowl. Add the yeast, honey, egg, and salt. Mix on low speed, or by hand with a wooden spoon or spatula, to combine. Add 1 cup of flour and mix to form a thick batter.

3. If using a stand mixer, switch to the dough hook and add the remaining 2½ cups flour, ½ cup at a time, until the dough gathers on the hook and begins to pull away from the side of the bowl. Knead

Continued

for 3-4 minutes to develop the dough. If mixing by hand, add the remaining flour until you can't stir anymore. You may not use all of the flour. Turn the dough out onto a lightly floured surface and knead until the dough is elastic but still soft, about 5-6 minutes.

4. Transfer the dough to an oiled bowl, turning once to coat, then cover with plastic wrap and let rise until doubled in volume, about 1 hour.

5. Brush a 9-by-5-inch loaf pan with olive oil, line the pan with a strip of parchment paper, then brush the paper with more olive oil.

TO MAKE THE FILLING

1. In a food processor, combine the garlic, sage, cheese, and olive oil, and process until a thick paste forms. Alternatively, mince the ingredients together until a paste forms.

2. Turn the dough out onto a lightly floured surface, and roll to a 16-by-16-inch square. If the dough starts pulling back, let it rest for 5 minutes, then continue rolling. Spread the filling over the dough. Use a pizza cutter or sharp knife to cut the rectangle into four 4-inch strips. Stack the strips, filling-side up. Cut the stacked strips into 4 equal squares.

3. Arrange the stacks, standing up, in the pan, making sure a plain dough side (without the filling) is facing each end of the pan. Cover the pan and let the dough rise for 1 hour; it should fill the pan.

4. Preheat the oven to 375°F.

5. Bake the bread for 40 to 45 minutes, or until well puffed and golden brown, and the temperature in the middle is 190°F to 200°F. Let cool in the pan for 5 minutes, then use the parchment paper to lift the bread from the pan. Serve warm. Tear off slices of bread and enjoy.

INGREDIENT TIP: Sour cream can be used in place of the Greek yogurt.

ROSEMARY & OLIVE FOCACCIA

Serves 12

Focaccia is different than pizza; focaccia dough is baked into a thicker slab that is full of big, irregular air bubbles. The crust should be very chewy. Then it needs just a sprinkling of herbs and a few choice toppings. You can use cherry tomatoes instead of olives, or sage instead of rosemary. Just resist the urge to use too many toppings, because focaccia should be all about the bread. DAIRY-FREE, NUT-FREE, VEGAN

PREP TIME: 30 minutes, plus 20 minutes for the dough to rest and 2 hours 30 minutes to 3 hours to rise
BAKE TIME: 25 to 30 minutes
EQUIPMENT: Mixing bowls, electric mixer (optional), wooden spoon or spatula, baking sheet, parchment paper or silicone baking mat, pastry brush

1¾ cups (14 ounces, 420 ml) warm water
1 packet (2¼ teaspoons, 7g) instant dry yeast
4 cups (20 ounces, 560g) all-purpose flour, divided
¼ cup (1.75 ounces, 52.5 ml) extra-virgin olive oil
1½ teaspoons table salt
2 pints black and green olives, roughly chopped
1 tablespoon roughly chopped fresh rosemary
1 teaspoon flaky sea salt

1. In the bowl of a stand mixer with the paddle attachment or in a large mixing bowl using a wooden spoon or spatula, combine the warm water with the yeast. Add 2 cups of flour and mix to combine. Cover the bowl with plastic wrap or a damp kitchen towel and let the batter rest for 20 minutes. Add the ¼ cup of oil and the table salt.

2. If using a stand mixer, switch to the dough hook and add the remaining 2 cups of flour. Knead on medium-low speed for 20 minutes. The dough will be quite sticky but should also be very stretchy. If working by hand, use a plastic scraper to help you knead the wet dough. Scrape the dough into a lightly oiled bowl, turning once to coat. Cover with plastic wrap or a damp kitchen towel and set aside in a warm place until doubled in volume, 1 hour and 30 minutes to 2 hours.

Continued

3. Lightly oil a baking sheet with olive oil. Carefully place the risen dough onto the oiled pan and flip to coat the dough. Use your fingers to spread the dough to about a ½-inch-thick square or rectangle.

4. Allow the dough to rise for about 1 hour, until a finger poked in the dough leaves a dimple.

5. Preheat the oven to 400°F.

6. Use your fingers to dimple the top of the dough all over. Press the chopped olives into the dough, spacing them evenly over the focaccia. Brush with olive oil and sprinkle with the rosemary and sea salt.

7. Bake for 25 to 30 minutes, or until the focaccia is puffed and golden brown.

8. Transfer the focaccia to a cutting board and brush with more olive oil. Serve warm.

TECHNIQUE TIP: If you have more time, you can make focaccia using the Low-Knead Bread method (see page 168). Instead of kneading the dough for 20 minutes, just set it aside in the refrigerator for 12 to 18 hours. Continue with the recipe the next day. The long, slow rise in the refrigerator will develop the gluten in the dough.

PIZZA DOUGH/ MARGHERITA PIZZA

Makes two 12- to 14-inch pizzas (16 slices total)

Just about everybody loves pizza, don't they? A great pizza starts with a great dough, and homemade pizza dough is surprisingly easy to make. This versatile dough can be rolled into a traditional pizza shape or folded over your choice of fillings to make a calzone. NUT-FREE

PREP TIME: 15 minutes, plus 1 hour for the dough to rise
BAKE TIME: 30 minutes
EQUIPMENT: Mixing bowl, electric mixer (optional), wooden spoon or spatula, rolling pin, baking sheets, pizza cutter

FOR THE DOUGH

1¼ cups (10 ounces, 275 ml) warm water
1 packet (2¼ teaspoons, 7g) instant dry yeast
3 cups (15 ounces, 400g) all-purpose flour, divided
2 tablespoons (1 ounce, 30 ml) extra-virgin olive oil
1 teaspoon salt

FOR THE PIZZA

Cornmeal, for dusting
3 cups of your favorite tomato sauce or 4 cups fresh tomato slices, drained on paper towels
1 pound fresh mozzarella cheese, sliced or shredded
1 large bunch fresh basil, leaves removed from the stems

TO MAKE THE DOUGH

1. In the bowl of a stand mixer with the paddle attachment or in a large mixing bowl using a wooden spoon or spatula, mix the water, yeast, and 1½ cups of flour until it looks like pancake batter.

2. If using a stand mixer, switch to the dough hook. Add the olive oil and salt. Add the remaining 1½ cups of flour, ¼ cup at a time, until the dough gathers on the hook and begins to pull away from the side of the bowl. Knead with the dough hook for 2 to 3 minutes. If mixing with a wooden spoon or spatula, add the remaining flour until you can't stir anymore, then finish kneading in the flour by hand.

3. Turn the dough out onto a lightly floured surface and knead into a smooth ball. Place the dough in a lightly oiled bowl and turn once to coat. Cover with plastic wrap or a damp kitchen towel and leave in a warm place until doubled in volume, about 1 hour.

Continued

TO MAKE THE PIZZA

1. Preheat the oven to 450°F.

2. Turn the dough out onto a lightly floured surface. Using a scraper or sharp knife, cut the dough into 2 equal pieces. Form each piece into a ball by tucking the sides under the dough. Using the tips of your fingers, flatten and press each piece of dough into a disk.

3. On a lightly floured surface, using a rolling pin, roll each piece of dough into a 12- to 14-inch round.

4. If you are using a baking stone, place each crust onto a wooden peel. Alternatively, use the back of a baking sheet sprinkled heavily with cornmeal.

5. Top each pizza with half each of the sauce or tomato slices, cheese, and basil leaves.

6. Bake one pizza at a time for 15 minutes, or until the crust is well browned and the cheese is melted and bubbling.

7. Use a pizza cutter to cut each pie into 8 slices.

VARIATION TIP: You can make whole-wheat pizza crust by substituting 1 cup of the all-purpose flour with whole-wheat flour. You can also vary the toppings according to your taste.

ZUCCHINI & RICOTTA PIE

Serves 8

This zucchini pie is a wonderful summertime recipe. The dough can be made way ahead, and all the components can be prepared early on the day you serve it. The pie can be eaten warm, at room temperature, or slightly chilled. Other than the crust, zucchini, and salt, all the other ingredients are optional, so use whichever spices, cheese, and meat you have available. This recipe is endlessly adaptable. NUT-FREE

PREP TIME: 45 minutes

BAKE TIME: 1 hour 20 minutes to 1 hour 30 minutes

EQUIPMENT: Rolling pin, deep-dish pie plate, aluminum foil, skillet

½ recipe Flaky Pie Dough (page 113)

1½ pounds (680g) zucchini

1½ teaspoons kosher salt or 1 teaspoon table salt, plus more for seasoning

6 slices bacon (8 ounces, 224g), cut into ½-inch pieces

1 large onion, chopped

2 cups chopped tomatoes

3 garlic cloves, minced

Freshly ground black pepper

8 ounces (226g) ricotta cheese

1 cup basil leaves, minced

½ cup (1.5 ounces, 42g) grated Parmesan cheese, divided

1 egg

½ cup (1 ounce, 30g) panko bread crumbs, divided

1. Preheat the oven to 375°F. Roll out the pie dough and place in a pie pan, fluting the edges with your fingers or a fork.

2. Using a fork, prick the bottom of the pie shell 10 to 12 times. Let rest in the refrigerator while you prepare the zucchini.

3. Trim the ends from the zucchini and cut into ⅛-inch thick slices. Toss the zucchini and salt, and set aside for 30 minutes. Rinse and drain the zucchini, then line in single layers on paper towels.

4. Remove the pie shell from the refrigerator. Line it with aluminum foil and fill with pie weights or dried beans. Bake the pie shell for about 20 minutes, or until the dough is baked through and just beginning to brown.

Continued

5. While the pie shell is baking, cook the bacon bits in a skillet until crisp and drain on a paper towel. Drain all but 1 tablespoon of the bacon fat from the pan. Add the onion to the pan, and sauté until soft and just beginning to brown. Add the tomatoes and garlic to the onion and cook until the consistency of a thick sauce. Season with salt and pepper to taste.

6. In a medium bowl, stir together the ricotta cheese, basil, and ¼ cup of Parmesan cheese. Season with salt and pepper to taste. Stir in the egg.

7. When the pie shell is baked, remove from the oven and reduce the oven temperature to 350°F. Sprinkle half of the bread crumbs across the bottom of the pie shell. Beginning at the outside edge of the pie shell, arrange a quarter of the zucchini slices in the pie shell in slightly overlapping concentric circles. Sprinkle one-third of the

bacon bits over the zucchini, then spread on about one-third of the tomato sauce, followed by one-third of the ricotta mixture.

8. Continue layering the remaining zucchini, bacon, tomato sauce, and ricotta mixture to fill the pie shell, ending with a layer of zucchini. Combine the remaining ¼ cup each of Parmesan and bread crumbs and sprinkle evenly over the top of the pie.

9. Bake for 1 hour to 1 hour and 10 minutes, or until the top of the pie is well browned and the juices are bubbling.

10. Let the pie cool for at least one hour before slicing so the juices can reabsorb. Serve warm or at room temperature.

VARIATION TIP: To make this a vegan recipe, replace the bacon, cheese, and egg with vegan products, or omit them altogether.

ROASTED VEGGIE PASTIES

Makes 8 pasties

This is a riff on traditional Cornish pasties, hand pies filled with meat and potatoes. For folks on the go, the pasty was a convenient lunch that could be filled with leftovers from last night's dinner and eaten without utensils. These pasties are filled with lots of roasted veggies and a Cheddar cheese sauce. Feel free to swap out the broccoli, onion, or mushrooms for your favorite veggies. NUT-FREE

PREP TIME: 45 minutes

BAKE TIME: 20 to 25 minutes

EQUIPMENT: Saucepan, whisk, baking sheets, parchment paper or silicone baking mats, mixing bowl, rolling pin, pastry brush

2 tablespoons (1 ounce, 30g) unsalted butter

2 tablespoons all-purpose flour

1 cup (8 ounces, 225 ml) whole milk

6 ounces (170g) Cheddar cheese, shredded

¼ teaspoon mustard powder or 1 teaspoon mustard

¼ teaspoon cayenne pepper (optional)

1 teaspoon salt, divided, plus more for seasoning

Freshly ground black pepper

1 bunch broccoli (about 12 ounces, 405g), cut into 1- to 1½-inch pieces

¼ cup (1.75 ounces, 52.5 ml) extra-virgin olive oil, divided

1 large onion, sliced

4 garlic cloves, minced

1 cup (3.5 ounces, 100g) mushrooms, sliced

1 recipe Flaky Pie Dough (page 113)

1 egg, beaten, for egg wash

Sesame seeds, for sprinkling

1. In a small saucepan, melt the butter. Add the flour and cook, stirring, to make a roux. Slowly whisk in the milk. Cook until the sauce thickens. Add the cheese, mustard, cayenne (if using), and salt and pepper to taste. Stir until the cheese is melted. Cover, remove from the heat, and let cool to room temperature.

2. Preheat the oven to 375°F.

3. Arrange the broccoli on a baking sheet. Drizzle with 2 tablespoons of olive oil and ½ teaspoon of salt. Toss to coat. Bake for about 10 minutes, until the florets are almost tender. Add the onion, garlic, and mushrooms, and toss to combine. Add more olive oil if the mixture is too dry, and add another ½ teaspoon salt. Bake for another 10 minutes, or until all the vegetables are crisp-tender. Remove the baking sheet from the oven and let the vegetables cool to room temperature.

Continued

4. Transfer the vegetables to a large bowl and mix in the cheese sauce. Taste and adjust the seasonings as needed.

5. Set the oven temperature to 400°F. Line two baking sheets with parchment paper or silicone baking mats.

6. Roll the dough ⅛ inch thick. Use a cookie cutter or a small plate as a guide to cut 6-inch rounds from the dough. Re-roll the scraps and continue cutting to use all the dough.

7. Brush the edge of each round with egg wash. Divide the filling among the rounds, using about ⅓ cup each.

8. Lift the two sides of the dough over the filling and pinch the edges to crimp. The crimped edges should be on the top of the pasty. Arrange the pasties, standing up, on the prepared baking sheets. Use a fork to poke steam vents on each side of the pasty. Brush with egg wash and sprinkle with sesame seeds.

9. Bake the pasties for 20 to 25 minutes, or until golden brown. Serve warm.

MAKE-AHEAD TIP: The dough, sauce, and vegetables can be made a day ahead, but don't mix the sauce with the vegetables until ready to assemble the pasties. You can roll and cut the dough rounds several days ahead or freeze for up to a month. The pasties are best eaten the day they're baked, but leftovers can be refrigerated or frozen and warmed in the oven to serve.

SAMOSAS

Makes 32 samosas

For Westerners, samosas are probably the most popular dish from Indian cuisine. These delicious little fried pastries are packed with flavorful potatoes and peas. This traditional recipe has a lengthy list of ingredients, but if you can't find every single one, no problem. Feel free to experiment with a variety of spices and flavorings. You can use lentils, meats, and even noodles or cheese to create your own filling. DAIRY-FREE, NUT-FREE (CAN BE MADE VEGAN: SEE INGREDIENT LIST)

PREP TIME: 45 minutes

COOK TIME: 30 to 40 minutes

EQUIPMENT: Mixing bowls, food processor, baking sheet, parchment paper or silicone baking mat, rolling pin, saucepan or skillet

FOR THE DOUGH

2 cups (10 ounces, 280g) all-purpose flour

½ teaspoon salt

⅓ cup (2.5 ounces, 75 ml) vegetable oil, plus more for frying

½ cup (4 ounces, 120 ml) water

FOR THE FILLING

3 or 4 medium (12 ounces, 340g) potatoes, peeled

¼ cup (1.75 ounces, 52.5 ml) vegetable oil

1½ teaspoons coriander seeds

1 teaspoon mustard seeds

1 teaspoon cumin seeds

1 tablespoon minced fresh ginger

1 garlic clove, minced

1 small jalapeño pepper, stemmed, seeded, and minced

1 teaspoon salt

1 teaspoon ground turmeric

½ teaspoon cayenne pepper, plus more for seasoning

½ teaspoon garam masala

½ cup frozen peas, cooked according to package directions

FOR THE CILANTRO DIPPING SAUCE

½ cup packed fresh cilantro leaves and tender stems

½ cup packed fresh mint leaves and tender stems

3 tablespoons freshly squeezed lemon juice

1 tablespoon vegetable oil

2 teaspoons granulated sugar (use organic sugar to make the recipe vegan)

1 small jalapeño or serrano pepper, stemmed and seeded

1 garlic clove

1 (½-inch) piece fresh ginger

½ teaspoon cumin seeds or ground cumin

Kosher salt

Continued

TO MAKE THE DOUGH

In a large mixing bowl, combine the flour and salt. Add the oil and use your fingers to rub it into the flour until it looks like coarse cornmeal. Add the water and knead the mixture into a smooth but firm dough. Cover the dough with plastic wrap or a damp kitchen towel and set aside while you make the filling, or refrigerate the dough overnight.

TO MAKE THE FILLING

1. Boil the potatoes in salted water until crisp-tender. Set aside to cool.

2. Heat the oil in a sauté pan. Add the coriander seeds, mustard seeds, and cumin seeds. Sauté over medium-high heat until the seeds become aromatic and lightly browned. Add the ginger, garlic, and jalapeño, and cook for a minute to soften the pepper. Remove the pan from the heat.

3. Dice the cooled potatoes smaller than ½ inch and place them in a mixing bowl. Fold in the spice mixture from the sauté pan, then add the salt, turmeric, cayenne, garam masala, and peas. Taste and adjust season with more cayenne if needed. Let the filling cool to room temperature or refrigerate overnight.

TO MAKE THE CILANTRO DIPPING SAUCE

In a food processor, combine the cilantro, mint, lemon juice, vegetable oil, sugar, jalapeño, garlic, ginger, cumin, and salt, and purée to a smooth paste.

TO ASSEMBLE AND FRY THE SAMOSAS

1. Divide the dough into 16 pieces. Line a baking sheet with parchment paper.

2. Roll one piece of dough into a 5- to 6-inch circle. Cut the circle in half. Pick up one half and brush lightly with water along the straight edge. Holding the half circle along either end of the straight edge, bring together the two sides to form a cone. Pinch along the seam to seal the cone. Scoop a tablespoon of the filling into the cone. Brush the inside edge of the dough with water and pinch the edge together to seal and transfer to the prepared baking sheet. Repeat this process with the remaining pieces of dough. Keep the samosas covered with a damp kitchen towel while you heat the oil.

3. In a heavy saucepan or skillet, heat 2 inches of vegetable oil to 375°F. Add a few samosas at a time to the oil, making sure not to overcrowd the pan. Adjust the heat to medium. Fry for 2 to 3 minutes on each side, or until golden brown.

4. Transfer the samosas to a wire rack as they finish frying and let drain.

5. Serve the samosas warm or room temperature, with the cilantro dipping sauce.

MAKE-AHEAD TIP: Assembled samosas can be frozen for up to three months. Let thaw at least halfway before frying.

BEEF & GUINNESS POTPIE

Serves 8

Looking for an easy, warm, and comforting meal idea? Here, a hearty beef stew is spiked with a full bottle of Guinness Stout, then baked in a flaky puff pastry crust. You can serve this dish with a pint of Guinness, of course! NUT-FREE

PREP TIME: 30 minutes

COOK TIME: 2 hours

BAKE TIME: 30 minutes

EQUIPMENT: Mixing bowl, lidded oven-safe pot, rolling pin, pastry brush

2 pounds (32 ounces, 900g) beef chuck or other stewing beef, cut into 1½-inch cubes

2 tablespoons all-purpose flour

¼ cup (1.75 ounces, 52.5 ml) vegetable oil, divided

1 large onion, diced

2 medium carrots, peeled and diced

2 celery stalks, sliced

2 parsnips, peeled and diced

1 teaspoon table salt, plus more for seasoning

1 bottle Guinness Stout beer

2 cups (16 ounces, 480 ml) water, beef stock, or chicken stock

1 bay leaf

2 teaspoons Worcestershire sauce

Freshly ground black pepper

½ recipe Quick Puff Pastry (page 144) or 1 sheet frozen puff pastry

1 egg, beaten, for egg wash

Flaky sea salt, for sprinkling

1. In a bowl, toss the beef cubes with the flour. Set aside.

2. In a large Dutch oven or heavy pot over medium-high, heat 2 tablespoons of oil.

3. Add half of the beef to the pot and reduce the heat to medium. Cook the meat on all sides until well browned, 10 to 15 minutes. Transfer the meat to a plate. Add more oil to the pot if needed, cook the rest of the meat until well browned on all sides, and transfer to the plate.

4. In the same pot, heat the remaining 2 tablespoons of oil. Add the onion, carrots, celery, and parsnips. Sprinkle 1 teaspoon of table salt over the vegetables. Cook, stirring often, until the vegetables begin to soften.

5. Pour the beer over the vegetables. Stir, scraping the bottom of the pot to loosen the brown bits. Return the browned meat to the pan. Add the water or stock, bay leaf, and Worcestershire sauce. The liquid should just barely cover the meat and vegetables. Bring the stew to a boil, then reduce heat to low.

6. Cover the pot and cook over low heat for about 2 hours, until the meat is very tender. The sauce should be thick enough to coat

the back of a spoon. If the sauce is too thin, uncover and let the liquid reduce. If the sauce is too thick, add a little more water or stock. Season to taste with salt and pepper. Turn off the heat, remove the bay leaf, and let the stock cool to room temperature. The stew can be refrigerated for up to 2 days before assembling the pie.

7. Pour the stew into a 13-by-9-inch lasagna pan.

8. On a work surface, roll the puff pastry to a 14-by-10-inch rectangle. Lay the pastry over the stew in the pan.

9. Cut three large slits in the middle of the pastry to vent. Brush the entire surface of the pastry with egg wash and sprinkle with sea salt.

10. Bake the potpie for about 30 minutes, or until the pastry is golden brown and puffed and the stew is hot. If the stew is cold from the refrigerator, it might take a little longer to bake. Serve immediately.

VARIATION TIP: Instead of puff pastry, you can top this potpie with Flaky Pie Dough (page 113) or unbaked Flaky Butter-milk Biscuits (page 201).

EMPANADAS

Makes 24 empanadas

Empanadas are a traditional part of cuisines across Latin America and in Spain. The name is derived from the Spanish *empanar*, which means to wrap or coat something in bread. Every region, country, and cook has their own version of empanadas. This recipe uses some of the most popular ingredients for the filling. NUT-FREE

PREP TIME: 45 minutes

BAKE TIME: 12 to 15 minutes

EQUIPMENT: Mixing bowls, whisk, baking sheets, parchment paper or silicone baking sheets, rolling pin, pastry brush

FOR THE DOUGH

3 cups (15 ounces, 420g) all-purpose flour

½ teaspoon salt

½ cup vegetable shortening

1 egg yolk

1 cup (8 ounces, 240 ml) whole milk

FOR THE FILLING

2 tablespoons (1 ounce, 30 ml) extra-virgin olive oil

1 medium onion, chopped

3 garlic cloves, minced

½ teaspoon salt, plus more for seasoning

½ teaspoon freshly ground black pepper, plus more for seasoning

1 tablespoon ground cumin

1 tablespoon sweet paprika

1 tablespoon dried oregano

¼ teaspoon cayenne pepper

1 pound (453g) ground beef

¾ cup (6 ounces, 180 ml) low-sodium or homemade chicken stock

½ cup (4 ounces, 112g) chopped scallions, white and green parts

½ cup (4 ounces, 112g) raisins

¼ cup (2 ounces, 56g) green olives, roughly chopped

1 egg, whisked, for egg wash

Flaky sea salt

TO MAKE THE DOUGH

1. In a large mixing bowl, mix the flour and salt. Add the shortening and use your fingers to work it into the flour until it looks like coarse cornmeal. In a separate bowl, whisk the egg yolk into the milk, then add that mixture to the flour. Stir just until the flour is absorbed. Turn the dough out onto a lightly floured work surface and knead briefly to bring the dough together.

2. The dough can be used immediately or wrapped in plastic and refrigerated for 1 to 2 days.

TO MAKE THE FILLING AND ASSEMBLE

1. Heat the olive oil in a sauté pan. Add the onion, garlic, and ½ teaspoon of salt. Cook until the onion softens. Add ½ teaspoon of black pepper, cumin, paprika, oregano, and cayenne. Cook for 1 minute to bloom the spices. Add the ground beef and cook until no longer pink. Stir in the stock. Stir in the scallions, raisins, and green olives. Turn off the heat and let cool to room temperature. The filling can be made the day before and refrigerated.

2. Preheat the oven to 375°F. Line two baking sheets with parchment paper or silicone baking mats.

3. On a lightly floured work surface, roll the dough ⅛ inch thick. Use a cookie cutter or a small plate as a guide to cut 4-inch rounds from the dough. Re-roll the scraps and continue cutting to use all the dough.

4. Brush the edge of each round with egg wash. Divide the filling among the rounds, using about 2 tablespoons of filling for each one.

5. Fold the dough over the filling and pinch the edges or use a fork to crimp. Arrange the empanadas on the prepared baking sheets. Use a fork to poke a steam vent on top of each empanada. Brush with egg wash and sprinkle with sea salt. Bake for 12 to 15 minutes, or until golden brown. Serve warm.

TECHNIQUE TIP: The empanadas can also be fried instead of baked. Assembled empanadas can be frozen for up to 3 months. Let thaw at last halfway before baking or frying.

Measurement Conversions

VOLUME EQUIVALENTS (LIQUID)

US STANDARD	US STANDARD (OUNCES)	METRIC (APPROXIMATE)
2 tablespoons	1 fl. oz.	30 mL
¼ cup	2 fl. oz.	60 mL
½ cup	4 fl. oz.	120 mL
1 cup	8 fl. oz.	240 mL
1½ cups	12 fl. oz.	355 mL
2 cups or 1 pint	16 fl. oz.	475 mL
4 cups or 1 quart	32 fl. oz.	1 L
1 gallon	128 fl. oz.	4 L

OVEN TEMPERATURES

FAHRENHEIT (F)	CELSIUS (C) (APPROXIMATE)
250°F	120°C
300°F	150°C
325°F	165°C
350°F	180°C
375°F	190°C
400°F	200°C
425°F	220°C
450°F	230°C

VOLUME EQUIVALENTS (DRY)

US STANDARD	METRIC (APPROXIMATE)
⅛ teaspoon	0.5 mL
¼ teaspoon	1 mL
½ teaspoon	2 mL
¾ teaspoon	4 mL
1 teaspoon	5 mL
1 tablespoon	15 mL
¼ cup	59 mL
⅓ cup	79 mL
½ cup	118 mL
⅔ cup	156 mL
¾ cup	177 mL
1 cup	235 mL
2 cups or 1 pint	475 mL
3 cups	700 mL
4 cups or 1 quart	1 L

WEIGHT EQUIVALENTS

US STANDARD	METRIC (APPROXIMATE)
½ ounce	15 g
1 ounce	30 g
2 ounces	60 g
4 ounces	115 g
8 ounces	225 g
12 ounces	340 g
16 ounces or 1 pound	455 g

Recipe Index

Index

Acknowledgments

First and foremost, thanks to Michèl, Catherine, and Joseph for always being supportive of my career and for being the three most important people in my life.

Thanks to my mother for being my biggest fan.

I am forever grateful to my late father for passing on his love of science. I treasure the memory of our long conversations about the chemistry of bread baking.

I appreciate my helpful neighbors who are always ready to take excess baked goods off my hands.

To my husband's coworkers, thanks for giving feedback on the recipes, and I'm sorry about any weight gain from the copious amount of carbs you ate during my recipe testing!

Thanks to the team at Callisto Media for guiding me through my first print cookbook.

About the Author

EILEEN GRAY is a pastry chef, blogger, and food writer. She has a degree in pastry arts from The Restaurant School at Walnut Hill College and a BA in English from West Chester University.

She gained wide experience in the pastry industry working for hotels, restaurants, bakeries, and caterers. From 2007 to 2016, she was the owner and pastry chef of Cake Art Studio, an award-winning custom cake bakery.

In 2015, Eileen launched her blog, Baking Sense, to share her love for baking and her years of pastry experience with home bakers around the world.

Eileen is married and has two grown children. She lives in the Philadelphia area.

CPSIA information can be obtained
at www.ICGtesting.com
Printed in the USA
BVHW090941111218
535251BV00016BA/133/P